READING FOR
YOUNG PEOPLE

THE SOUTHEAST

READING
FOR YOUNG PEOPLE

THE
SOUTHEAST

DOROTHY HEALD,
Regional Editor

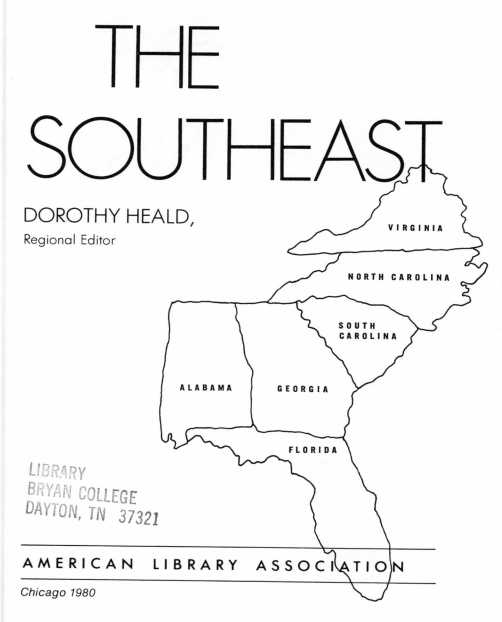

AMERICAN LIBRARY ASSOCIATION

Chicago 1980

READING FOR YOUNG PEOPLE

A series of annotated bibliographies of fiction and nonfiction titles, compiled for readers from the primary grades through the tenth grade and designed to focus on the history and character of each region of these United States.

THE MIDWEST by *Dorothy Hinman and Ruth Zimmerman*

Edited by *F. Laverne Carroll*, The University of Oklahoma, Norman
  THE GREAT PLAINS by *Mildred Laughlin*
  THE ROCKY MOUNTAINS by *Mildred Laughlin*
  THE MIDDLE ATLANTIC by *Arabelle Pennypacker*

Library of Congress Cataloging in Publication Data

Heald, Dorothy W
    The Southeast, an annotated bibliography.

    (Reading for young people)
    Includes index.
    1. Southern States—Juvenile literature—Bibliography.
2. Southern States—Bibliography.   3. Southern States—
Juvenile fiction—Bibliography.   I. Title.   II. Series.
Z1251.S7H4   [F209]   016.975   80-16137
ISBN 0-8389-0300-2

Printed in the United States of America

CONTENTS

ACKNOWLEDGMENTS

This publication has been made possible by the dedicated efforts of the six state editors, each of whom brought to the task a wide knowledge of the literature of his or her state, expertise in evaluating that literature's appeal to students, and the ability to communicate an author's style and message through interesting annotations. These editors are: Ruth Waldrop, Assistant Professor, Graduate School of Library Science, University of Alabama; Bill Taylor, Supervisor of Educational Media, Hillsborough County Public Schools, Tampa, Florida; Grace Hightower, recently retired Director of School Libraries, Georgia State Department of Education; Willie Boone, retired librarian, Durham, North Carolina, and Donna Heald, graduate of Appalachian State University, Boone, North Carolina, and currently Media Specialist, Piper High School, Fort Lauderdale, Florida; Margaret Ehrhardt and Mary Frances Griffin, Library Consultants, South Carolina Department of Education, assisted by graduate students in the College of Librarianship, University of South Carolina; Christina Dunn and Sara Crews, Supervisors for School Libraries, Department of Education, Commonwealth of Virginia.

Dr. Frances Laverne Carroll, Series Editor and Professor of Library Science at the University of Oklahoma, currently serving as Visiting Professor and Senior Lecturer, Library Studies Department, Western Australian Secondary Teachers College, and Mr. Herbert Bloom, Senior Editor, American Library Association, contributed to the planning of the series and assisted in the preparation of the manuscript.

Special appreciation goes to the kind librarians in the Watuaga County Library, Boone, North Carolina, and the State Library of Florida, in Tallahassee, for the generous assistance they gave me during the compilation of this publication.

Dorothy Heald
Regional Editor

INTRODUCTION

Today's increased interest in our national heritage and its regional components has created a need for an up-to-date comprehensive list of books of literary quality which would serve to supplement the rather meager listings found as part of the courses-of-study prepared for state history in the various states, or the brief listings of materials which comprise part of units-of-study on various regions of the United States. These are usually limited to factual materials, thus ignoring the well-done fiction that presents an accurate account of scenes and conditions characteristic of the area. The purpose of this southeast regional bibliography is threefold:

1. To introduce the young people living in the southeast region to books dealing with their unique cultural heritage
2. To help young people in other regions of the United States become more aware of the historical and social influences that have shaped the lives of those living in the Southeast
3. To serve as a selection tool for librarians, teachers, and students as they plan for units-of-work or special projects in which the southeast regional culture is identified.

When reference is made to the southeastern United States, often called "the deep South," the states usually cited are Alabama, Florida, Georgia, North and South Carolina, and Virginia. These states share many of the same geographical and cultural attributes, while varying sufficiently in other areas, to make an interesting regional pattern. Historical backgrounds of each state contain many similarities, but current life-styles vary greatly from state to state. Black culture has deep roots in this section of our country and is well represented on the appropriate state lists. Spanish-American, Cuban-American, and other ethnic cultural heritages may be found in the literature of these states, as will the old-English traditions found in the Appalachian region. Interesting historical fiction will give students a glimpse of life in the early days of our country, while more modern literature will help them appreciate the growth and development of the states in this region. The emphasis for the total work is on creative literature—fiction, biography, folklore, poetry, drama—with less attention paid to general informational books from such disciplines as social science, geography, science, and history.

Selection criteria includes literary quality, accuracy of detail, true regional feeling and description, and appropriateness for the grade level being targeted. Out-of-print titles are included when a very valuable approach is not available in another work, and when copies of the work are generally found in libraries across the country. In this way the user of the bibliography will be alerted to the value of the work, with the result that more use will be made of the material and unwarranted discarding will be avoided.

Each entry includes complete bibliographical data followed by an original annotation. A brief quotation from each book is given to identify the author's unique style, the theme, strong characterization, or mood of the work. Then a brief descriptive resume indicating the book's content, scope, regional value, and style is combined with a critical evaluation of the merits of the work. The limitations, if any, may involve comparisons with other titles on the same subject or other works by the same author. A suggestion for special use or identification of a section appropriate for arousing interest in the book is included when appropriate. The bibliographic data also includes suggested general grade ranges—primary (P), intermediate (I), junior high (J), senior high (S)—to aid the user in selecting materials appropriate for a specific level.

The bibliography does not pretend to be all-inclusive, but includes those titles which the editors felt best exemplified their own region's characteristics. It is arranged alphabetically by author within the general areas of Fiction; Folktales; Poetry, Drama and Music; Biography and Personal Accounts; and Other Informational Books. Illustrators other than the author of the work are included in the bibliographical data.

An author-title-subject index to the bibliography's entries is provided. The entry number is the key used in the index for locating entries. Specific pagination is included for nonfiction works in which three or more pages deal with a specific subject.

A list of the books submitted by each state editor is located in the

State lists, alphabetically arranged by author within the broad areas of the bibliography. The number preceding each entry identifies the matching annotation. Some titles may appear on more than one list since some works cover material on several states.

For the convenience of the users of the bibliography, the addresses of publishers not listed in *Books in Print,* or those of particular local importance, are found following the state lists. If some out-of-print books are still available within the state, that source is also noted.

It is the hope of all those engaged in the preparation of this work that it will serve to give many students a new look at the southeastern region of their country and lead them to a greater interest in and appreciation for its history, its culture, and its beauty. Happy reading!

ANNOTATED BIBLIOGRAPHY

FICTION

1   Allen, Merritt Parmelee. *Johnny Reb.*   Illus. by   (J, S)
     Ralph Ray, Jr. Longmans, 1952. 250p.

> . . . provide him with a mount and outfit and teach him how to use them.

The Civil War was beginning and Ezra, unschooled in everything, wanted to get into Colonel Wade Hampton's Legion and fight with the man he worshipped. Colonel Hampton sent an old friend out for five days with Ezra to teach him how to ride; they soon were on their way North to join General Beauregard's forces. The story, most interestingly told by Allen, is fair to both sides and well written. It came as a surprise to Ezra that the "Yanks" were just as eager to get back home as he was, and it was even more surprising to him when he found his wounded relative, who was a soldier on the other side of the battle line. An easy-to-read story told in such an interesting fashion that adults as well as younger readers will enjoy it.

2   Armstrong, William H. *Sounder.*   Illus. by James   (I, J)
     Barkley. Harper, 1969. 116p.

> The old coon dog would lie facing his master, with his one eye fixed and his one ear raised.

This is the story of the coon dog, Sounder, and his devotion to his master. At the same time it is the story of the father, a black sharecropper who must steal to feed his family; the timid mother fighting for survival; the son who grows to maturity through his father's prison term; and the devotion of Sounder. The characters are real and unforgettable in this deeply moving, long-ago story of loneliness, cruelty, and silent suffering.

3   Ball, Zachary.   *Salvage Diver.*   Holiday House, 1961.   (I, J, S)
    220p.

> It uncovered something else. He was looking directly into the expressionless eyes of a tiger shark!

Joe Panther, the Seminole Indian charter boat captain, and his mate, Tiger Tail, accept a job looking for salvageable shipwrecks in the Florida Keys. Joe's close call with the tiger shark is just one of their many underwater adventures. Lots of fast-paced skin diving action in authentic settings, careful attention to the aspects of diving and salvage, and vivid description of marine life and the natural history of the sea, add up to entertaining reading and some painless incidental learning.

4   Banning, Margaret Culkin.   *I Took My Love to the*   (S)
    Country.   Harper, 1966.   250p.

> The road narrowed and began to curve, to mount little hills and dip into valleys.

The setting of this romantic novel of the late 1950s moves from New York City to one of the small mountain towns of North Carolina where Jenny and Stephen Cooper hope to rebuild their failing marriage and find a more secure life-style. Today's teenagers may question the sexist attitudes expressed in the female characterization, but they are true to the trends of the times being portrayed. The vivid descriptions of the countryside, the authenticity of manners and customs, and the realistic characterizations of the inhabitants serve to give students a glimpse into one of the most charming regions of the state.

5   Bannon, Laura.   *When the Moon is New: a Seminole*   (P, I)
    Indian Story.   Whitman, 1953.   unp.

> The air was full of mystery. Little Rainbow Jumper could feel it all around her.

The small Seminole Indian girl was told by her mother that she would find out what the mystery was when the moon was new. In the meantime she was to visit relatives in another village, helping to care for a baby cousin. On returning to her own village, she learned that the mystery was not her own sewing machine as she had hoped but something far more exciting. The author's colorful and realistic illustrations add much to this charming story of a simpler way of life and a less complex time in America's history.

6   Baughman, Dorothy. *Piney's Summer.* Illus. by   (P, I)
Tom Allen.   Coward, 1976.   70p.

Piney's world was small, but just now he felt right on top of it.

Drawn in part from the childhood experiences of the author who lived in Eclectic, Alabama, this is an easy-to-read collection of adventures that portray the variety and exciting experiences during a summer in the life of a small Alabama boy.

7   Beaman, Joyce Proctor.   *All for the Love of Cassie.*   (J, S)
Moore, 1973.   119p.

I was awakened from my daydreams with shouts from Freddie that his biddies were hatching.

Cassie Beckton is a typical fourteen-year-old girl, engrossed in helping her family (Mama, Papa, and four-year-old brother Freddie) with chores on the tobacco farm. After the death of her father, the struggle to keep the farm, while finishing high school and working as a nurse's aide in the local hospital, requires a great deal of courage and strength. Local customs, neighborhood relationships, and some typical farm life experiences of the period are realistically described in this easy-to-read love story set in eastern North Carolina during the 1930s depression.

8   Beaman, Joyce Proctor.   *Broken Acres.*   John F.   (J, S)
Blair.   1971.   145p.

The broiling sun drew from the earth enough moisture to sicken the air.

Melody Nottoman, the twelve-year-old daughter of a tobacco farmer in Wilson, North Carolina, was deeply concerned over her little brother Teddy's deformed ear. This story of her efforts to interest an ear doctor in Teddy's problem is an exciting adventure which gives a realistic picture of the life on a tobacco farm in the 1950s.

9   Beatty, John Louis, and Beatty, Patricia.   *Who Comes*   (J, S)
to King's Mountain?   Morrow, 1975.   287p.

I am not Duncan, Father. I don't want to be a soldier.

Young Alec McLeod was torn between the view of his loyalist father and his own dislike of war and killing. As the Redcoats returned to retake the colony of South Carolina, Alec struggled to find where his loyalties lay and to establish his own identity. Living in the primarily Highland Scots community of Ninety-Six Section, Alec was an unquestioning king's man. However, after witnessing the hanging of his rebel grandfather, the murder of a friend, and an attack on his own father by the king's men, Alec ran away to join Francis Marion and his Swamp Rats. This exciting novel of the American Revolution not only traces the fortunes of Alec McLeod, but also vividly portrays the life and culture of the Highland Scottish settlers in South Carolina. Both the historical and fictional characters are presented in a clear and vivid manner, and the time span ranges from the taking of Charles Towne in 1780 to the Battle of King's Mountain.

10   Beim, Lorraine.   *Triumph Clear.*   Harcourt, 1946.   (I, J)
      200p.

    She couldn't contemplate her career any further. Her hopes, her thoughts, were too tender to be brought into the light of day.

A young girl, confidently planning on college and a dramatic career, is stricken with infantile paralysis. This is the story of her long struggle against discouragement. Marsh's struggle against polio should assist the reader regardless of the crisis which sooner or later one faces. The scene is the Georgia Warm Springs Foundation, and it acquaints the reader with the methods and progress of the foundation at the time of the writing.

11   Bell, Thelma Harrington.   *The Two Worlds of Davy*   (I, J)
      Blount.   Illus. by Corydon Bell.   Viking, 1962.   220p.

    From that day on there would be no quarrel in Grandmother's mind between the sea and the mountains.

Davy had lived all his ten years in the village of Hatteress on the Outer Banks of North Carolina, but he constantly heard his mountain-born granny extolling the beauty of "her mountains." The seashore, an old lighthouse, and stories of pirate's treasure, plus work on his grandfather's fishing boat filled his life until grandmother arranged a trip to the mountains for him. Realistic descriptions of both mountains and sea, artistic line drawings by the author's husband, and a good story make this an excellent resource for young readers.

12   Bell, Thelma Harrington.   *Yaller-Eye.*   Illus. by   (P, I)
      Corydon Bell.   Viking, 1951.   88p.

    Long, low clouds blew in out of the southwest and loosed their moisture in a heavy downpour when they struck the cool mountains.

When Yaller-Eye, Randy's rangy, orange-and-white cat, disappeared everyone was upset. Randy's experiences as he looked for her make an exciting story which is well illustrated with Corydon Bell's pencil drawings. Descriptions of the mountain setting and conversations using local idioms and folksongs give the reader a realistic picture of life in the Blue Ridge mountain area of North Carolina.

13   Blackburn, Joyce.   *Suki and the Magic Sand Dollar.*   (P, I)
Illus. by Stephanie Clayton.   Word Books, 1969.
62p.

From a saffron bow on the horizon, the moon had blossomed into a
perfect sphere.

Little Suki invites us to observe and learn with her about the wonders around us. She learns many exciting scientific facts during a visit
to Saint Simons Island, off the coast of Georgia. She watches the sea-
birds dive for fish, smells the salty air, goes to sleep listening to the tide
come in—"the waves rhythmical and booming." It is not until Suki
meets Cherry, a "real scientist," that she discovers the built-in clocks of
nature. Facts are interestingly presented as they are discovered by an
appealing little girl.

14   Blassingame, Wyatt.   *The Golden Geyser.*   (S)
Doubleday, 1961.   335p.

We're going to sell lots like Bennett plows. We're going to advertise
in New York and Chicago . . .

Reluctantly, young Bob Nelson gets caught up in the Florida real
estate boom of the 1920s, when fortunes were made overnight, only to
be lost just as quickly in the collapse which inevitably followed. Interwoven with fictional flappers and wheeler-dealers are equally colorful
actual Florida magnates such as Henry Flagler and Carl Fisher. Skillful blending of fact and fiction paints a vivid and entertaining picture
of an important era in Florida history.

15   Bodie, Idella.   *Ghost in the Capitol.*   Illus. by Mary   (I, J)
Arnold Garvin.   Sandlapper Press, 1973.   118p.

Was the ghost watching her? Did he know who had the lock of hair?

Inspired by a current event reported in a social studies class,
three children with their cat, Beelzebub, set out to solve the mystery
of the "bumping" in the state capitol building. These happenings had
been causing security officers to quit their jobs. The young detectives
planned to spend the night in the deserted building and to provide a
service for the state by exorcising the ghost. Historical events are
brought in through conversation, and incidental information on poltergeists and haunted houses is given.

16   Bodie, Idella.   *The Mystery of the Pirate's Treasure.*   (I, J)
Illus. by Louise Yancey.   Sandlapper Press, 1973.
136p.

It's a treasure! A pirate's treasure!

As Chris, Mike, and their mother started on their journey to

Charleston, no one thought that Chris would help solve a mystery. A clue to Steve Bonnet's treasure was found by Chris with the help of a mysterious man who followed him. After much searching and numerous frightening events, Chris and Mike located the treasure. During their adventure the two boys visited many places of interest in the port city of Charleston. The descriptions of historical places there are especially well done.

17   Bodie, Idella.   *The Secret of Telfair Inn.*   Illus. by   (I, J)
         Louise Yancey.   Sandlapper Press, 1971.   98p.

> Crawling through the vine-covered window, they found themselves on an aged stone terrace.

The summer that Phil and Marcy spent in Aiken, while their father was doing historical research in South Carolina, gave them a chance to do some exploring on their own. The old inn and its environs provided them with exciting adventures, new friends, and happy excursions into local history. When Telfair Inn was destined for demolition and Mr. Crowe, the caretaker, met with an accident, the children were involved in solving the mystery surrounding the old inn.

18   Bothwell, Jean.   *Lady of Roanoke.*   Holt, 1965.   (S)
         254p.

> He set Virginia down, smoothed the curls round her face and pulled her muslin cap straight.

Based on findings from oral traditions and private journals, Ms. Bothwell has taken characters from her earlier book, *Lost Colony,* and created this exciting story of Virginia Dare, the first English child born in America. Led by their Indian friend, Manteo, Virginia and her colonist friends immigrated to present-day North Carolina where they lived as wards of the Coree tribe. With a great deal of help from their Indian friends they learned to farm the land and establish a colony of their own. Documentation of the work is given in the foreword, the epilogue, and a four-page bibliography.

19   Boyd, James.   *Drums.*   Illus. by N. C. Wyeth.   (S)
         Scribner, 1925.   436p.

> The Gunner blew the steel dust from a flat file and squinted at Johnny's makeshift costume over his iron spectacles.

Johnny Fraser, born in frontier North Carolina and educated as a gentleman in colonial Edenton, must choose between the superficial English society he has adopted and his native American culture. Unable to resolve his inner conflicts, Johnny accepts his father's offer of honorable escape to England, never dreaming that his flight will carry him into the midst of the fighting on both land and sea. Action, descriptions of both colonial and London society, and strong characterizations highlight this account of the American Revolution.

20   Boyd, James. *Old Pines and Other Stories.* Univ. of   **(S)**
    North Carolina Pr., 1952. 165p.

    The old man's blunt figure at the base of a slender, quiet column stood out sharp and motionless.

James Boyd is an author and poet well-known for his historical fiction. This collection of short stories centering around small Southern towns is proof of his mastery of the short story as well. His understanding of the people, their ways, and their relationships is evident. Although the black/white social patterns are obviously those of the post-Civil War era, the people do not seem stereotyped but instead reflect genuine attitudes that have carried over even into some areas today. This first collection of Boyd's stories shows the wide range of the author's abilities to create impressions of a region, as well as of a way of life.

21   Bristow, Gwen. *Celia Garth.* Crowell, 1959. 460p.   **(J, S)**

    Be gentle, Celia. Be understanding. You've got a rough road ahead of you.

As a young orphan apprenticed in a Charleston sewing shop in 1779, Celia Garth had a rough road ahead. Caught in the bombardment and seige of the town, bereaved by her fiance's murder by Tarleton and his Green Dragoons, and enmeshed in the intrigue of spying for the Swamp Fox, Francis Marion, Celia endured much. The story depicts the scars of war which were inflicted on the city of Charleston and in the life of one young girl, Celia. This is an engrossing saga which reflects the agony of the Revolution in South Carolina.

22   Brothers, Betty. *Triggerfish: Tales of the Florida*   **(J, S)**
    Keys. Illus. by Netannis Kline. Wake-Brook House,
    1975. 154p.

    A soft breeze greeted us. Blowing off an endless expanse of sparkling, island-dotted aquamarine water.

The Florida Keys are a unique part of the United States, and an equally unique background for literature. This collection of short stories by a resident of the Keys presents the reader with an assortment of moods and topics, varied and changing as the hues of the waters surrounding the Keys. There is something in this collection for every taste: fantasy and grim reality, beauty and cruelty, nature and humanity. Stark pen-and-ink drawings capture the flavor of the locale as well as the stories.

23   Brown, Joe David. *Paper Moon.* Bantam, 1972.   (J, S)
      240p.

> I know you've heard about the Depression. Well, I don't think times
> were nearly so bad as some people put on.

Formerly titled *Addie Pray,* the story tells of an eleven-year-old
sassy orphaned girl traveling with a wheeler-dealer, Long Boy. Their
journeys, exploits, and adventures take place in rural Alabama during
the depression. Addie and Long Boy have charm and vitality. She is
a pint-sized frontier girl—tough, gritty, and fiercely protective of
Long Boy. The story is humorous and fast-paced.

24   Brown, Marion Marsh. *The Silent Storm.* Illus. by   (I, J)
      Fritz Kredel.   Abingdon, 1963.   250p.

> Annie smiled, not only because of Helen's comment, but also because
> things were so different from that other day long ago.

The journey to Tuscumbia, Alabama, to take care of the young
Keller child is the beginning of this story of Annie Sullivan Macy. In
flashbacks Annie remembers her own childhood, which helps her as
she works with the blind and deaf Helen Keller.

25   Brown, Marion Marsh. *The Swamp Fox.*   (I, J)
      Westminster, 1950.   185p.

> If he went adventuring, it would be only in defense of something
> dear to him.

Tirelessly devoted to the land settled by his Huguenot grandfather, disillusioned by the prevailing indifference and incompetence
of the military, Francis Marion, with his small band of soldiers and dis-
possessed planters, helped bring about the turning point in South Carolina's struggle to loosen the British occupation during the revolutionary
war. This fictionalized biography favorably portrays this early propo-
nent of hit-and-run guerrilla tactics as he matures from an adventurous
youth into a dedicated farmer, a respected officer in the regiment, and,
finally, into the wounded, hunted fighter who used sheer audacity
coupled with intimate knowledge of the marshlands to exasperate the
British and earn his infamous nickname. The author depicts the tumult
of the Revolution in South Carolina when farms rotted in neglect, loyalties were uncertain, and the old etiquette of battle no longer brought
victory.

26   Brown, Virginia Pounds. *The Gold Disc of Coosa.*   (I)
      Strode, 1975.   121p.

> You know the ways of our people. You have defied Seekaboo.

In search of the giant king called Taskaloosa, De Soto captures the city of Coosa in the present state of Alabama. The life of Utina, a sixteen-year-old Indian boy, changes dramatically during the occupation. The book climaxes with the battle of Maubaila, fought in 1540, the first important encounter between white men and Indians in the New World.

27 Burch, Robert. *D. J.'s Worst Enemy*. Illus. by Emil   (I)
    Weiss. Viking, 1965. 152p.

> Don't let's discourage him if he has finally decided that he wants to be a part of the family.

In the peach country of Georgia, D. J. Madison lives the joys of boyhood with his sidekick, Nutty, and the neighboring Casper boys. He teases his younger brother, Renfroe, and his older sister, Clara May, until they share a secret; D. J. feels left out. As D. J. changes, he learns to appreciate his family and realizes he is his own worst enemy. This true-to-life family story, told in the first person, is set during the 1930s.

28 Burch, Robert. *Hut School and the Wartime Home-*   (I)
    front. Illus. by Ronald Himler. Viking, 1974. 140p.

> Some . . . served coffee and doughnuts in the canteen at Terminal Station; some rolled bandages. . . .

The experiences and reactions of Kate Coleman and her sixth-grade classmates form the basis for this World War II story. The children learn about the war, its sorrows, and its effects on their lives. The appeal of the book is its authentic portrait of the period and the growing understanding of the children as to what war means. Included are plenty of lively incidents and some local Georgia color.

29 Burch, Robert. *Queenie Peavy*. Illus. by Jerry   (I, J)
    Lazore. Viking, 1966. 159p.

> If I'd been throwing at her, I'd have hit her. I've got better aim than 'most anybody.

Lonely thirteen-year-old Queenie Peavy has a chip on her shoulder—her schoolmates neglect her, her idolized father is in jail, and her mother works long hours in the mill. Life is difficult, but Queenie's character sees her through the dark days. Queenie is so real that the reader becomes deeply involved in everything that concerns her. This appealing story of a real tomboy gives a good picture of life in a small Georgia town during the depression years.

30 Burch, Robert. *Renfroe's Christmas*. Illus. by Rocco   (I)
    Negri. Viking, 1968. 59p.

13

Well, I believe I like getting presents best . . . no matter what's more blessed.

In spite of such statements, eight-year-old Renfroe is aware he is selfish. After half-hearted attempts to change, he suddenly and spontaneously gives away "the finest thing I have ever owned"—his new Mickey Mouse watch—to a retarded boy because it made him smile. A well-written story of Christmas in rural northern Georgia during the depression years, *Renfroe's Christmas* is filled with real people. The rural regional quality of the story is strong, the conversations brisk and abounding with poignancy. The details of the church pageant and party are told with humor.

31   Burch, Robert. *Simon and the Game of Chance.*   (I)
      Illus. by Fermin Rocker. Viking, 1970. 128p.

"Forget it, regret it," thought Simon, wondering if the preacher had even noticed the rhyme.

The above quotation shows how Simon's sense of humor and love of fun were ever present and often the cause of his difficulties. Simon, aged thirteen, is a member of a large family which is dominated by a religious, disciplinarian father who frowns on frivolity, card games, and such. The plot features a series of tragedies and Simon's conflicts with his father. As the family crises resolve themselves, Simon's father mellows a bit and Simon understands him a little better. The story concerns genuine interpersonal problems, which are discussed in a very interesting way.

32   Burch, Robert. *Skinny.* Illus. by Don Sibley.   (I)
      Viking, 1964. 127p.

Skinny looked away from her. "I sure don't look forward to leaving this hotel."

A sociable twelve-year-old orphan boy is given a home by the proprietor of a small town hotel in Georgia. Skinny wins the affection of everyone through his sincerity and innocently humorous outlook on life. This delightful story offers insight into life in a small town in rural Georgia during the 1930s.

33   Burch, Robert. *Tyler, Wilkin, and Skee.* Illus. by   (I)
      Don Sibley. Viking, 1963. 156p.

Oh, we'll stir around the old fairground and see what's going on.

The refrain above is what Skee sang all week, but it is eleven months later that he and his friends finally made it to the fair. Tyler, Wilkin, and Skee are three typical boys growing up in rural Georgia during the depression. The book relates their lives and antics during a full year from September through August. Although the central characters are boys, the story appeals to girls as well.

34   Burchard, Peter. *Bimby*. Coward, 1968. 91p.   (I)

    Jesse, where would you fly if you had wings?

The true meaning of Jesse's reply and how Bimby works out his own solution makes for interesting reading. Bimby is a young slave in the Sea Islands of Georgia just before the Civil War. His is the story of a growing boy thrust toward manhood by an unforeseen event. The black-and-white illustrations by the author enhance the story. The map frontispiece assists the reader in identifying places in the story—places which are still visited and enjoyed by many.

35   Burchard, Peter. *Rat Hell*. Coward, 1971. 61p.   (I, J)

    The system was simple. Only two men worked at once.

Jim Cutter was one of the twenty Yankee officers digging a tunnel to escape Libby Prison in Richmond, Virginia. Against armed guards and a complex of earthworks surrounding the city, the prisoners, driven by desperation, devised an ingenious plan of escape. Based on fact, the novel takes the reader through the events of that fateful night.

36   Burton, Herbert. *Adventures of Dixie North*. Illus.   (I)
    Gadsden, 1976. 217p.

    I lay down with my head at the tent flags and watched the clouds as they passed overhead.

Dixie North, an eleven-year-old stranded orphan, is a lovable, adventurous boy who longs for love and the assurance of belonging to someone. He and his friend, Chuck Hill, play in the Alabama countryside—swimming, riding, camping, and doing all the things boys do to make their days exciting as well as sometimes dangerous. Chuck's mother guesses Dixie's secret and helps him through some rough spots. This is a story full of laughter, excitement, strife, and mystery which will appeal to young readers.

37   Butterworth, W. E. *Dateline—Talladega*. Grosset,   (I, J)
    1972. 155p.

    You don't mean to tell me that you no longer want to be a lawyer . . .?

A. J. Morgan, a freshman in college, interested in becoming a lawyer, wins a summer internship with the Allied Press Association. His experiences in the newspaper office and covering automobile races at Talledega and other tracks in the state help firm his career goals.

38   Butterworth, W. E.   *The Roper Brothers and Their*   (J, S)
      Magnificent Steam Automobile.   Four Winds, 1976.
      218p.

> All of a sudden, very slowly, creaking, the Doble moved out of the little room.

Richard Roper, a seventeen-year-old farm boy from the Florida Panhandle, and his brother find a 1927 Doble Steam Roadster stored in the barn. Richard and his grandfather restore the car to running condition. Considerable detail about the construction and working of a steam car, an authentic and contemporary setting, well-drawn characters, an ample dash of humor, and an easy-to-read style add up to absorbing reading for automobile buffs and other teens as well.

39   Caras, Roger.   *Panther!*   Illus. by Charles Frane.   (J, S)
      Little, 1969.   185p.

> It was a time like all others in the Everglades, a time of life and death. . . .

The life of a Florida panther (mountain lion) was a struggle for survival in the primeval wilderness of the Everglades, where his natural enemies were few but deadly: the rattlesnake, the black bear, and the alligator. Deadliest of all was man—men such as Doc Painter, the professional lion hunter, and Will, the young rancher whose final encounter with Panther had tragic results. Caras blends the storyteller's art with the naturalist's science in this enjoyable nature novel.

40   Carroll, Ruth, and Carroll, Latrobe.   *Beanie.*   Walck,   (P)
      1953.   unp.

> All those noises told Beanie that everybody on the mountain farm was busy.

Beanie, the youngest member of the Tatum family, is having a birthday. More than anything he wants his very own little dog. When his father gives him a fat little puppy, Beanie leaves his job of carrying stovewood to the kitchen and goes out to see the world. His adventure takes him up the mountain where the bears live and into plenty of exciting situations before he finds his way home again. Ruth Carroll's delightful illustrations give additional glimpses of North Carolina mountain scenes. A good book for read-aloud time.

41   Cather, Willa.   *Sapphira and the Slave Girl.*   Knopf,   (S)
      1940.   295p.   (Paperback ed., Random, 1975)

> She had known her mother to show kindness to her servants, and, sometimes, cold cruelty.

Sapphira married beneath her station and moved to a backwoods Virginia farm. She owned slaves and was usually kind to them until she imagined a relationship between her husband and Nancy, a pretty young slave girl. Sapphira plotted Nancy's downfall, but Sapphira's daughter befriended Nancy and helped her escape to Canada and freedom. The book presents a good picture of life in Virginia prior to the Civil War.

42   Choate, Florence, and Curtis, Elizabeth. *The Five*   (J)
      Gold Sovereigns; A Story of Thomas Jefferson's Time.   op
      Illus.   Frederick A. Stokes, 1943.   207p.

    With honor we serve!

The family of Anne Farnsworth had always been loyal to the king, and her father and grandfather still supported the king. Therefore, Anne became confused when she heard her brother and young Thomas Jefferson speaking of independence for the colonies. The sovereign Anne wore around her neck to remind her of her responsibilities was her greatest treasure. However, she sent it to George Washington for his troops because she wanted to be a true "American."

43   Cleaver, Vera, and Cleaver, Bill. *Trial Valley.*   (J, S)
      Lippincott, 1977.   158p.

    Into our lives there came . . . a little shirttail boy we found abandoned near Trial Creek. . . .

After the deaths of her parents, as related in the author's earlier book, *Where the Lilies Bloom,* Mary Call Luther takes the responsibility of raising seven-year-old Ima Dean and twelve-year-old Romey. Mary Call has been raised to hard work and she tries to teach "her kids" these values as well as a respect for education. However, she finds her life complicated by conflicts with an older, married sister and must struggle to find a way to reconcile her traditional beliefs with her desire to improve their way of life. As in their former work, the Cleavers have described the values and traditions which are the basis of the mountain folk life-style: hard work, family and personal pride, self-reliance, and respect for the land.

44   Coatsworth, Elizabeth. *The Golden Horseshoe.*   (I, J)
      Illus. by Robert Lawson.   Macmillan, 1968.   153p.

    It was the wilderness that laid down the terms under which he might be allowed to live.

Governor Spotswood and his small band of followers from the Tidewater section find many differences in terrain, plant life, and animal life as they make their way closer to the great valley of Virginia. Tamar, disguised as an Indian lad, accompanies the knights of the Golden Horseshoe and Roger, her half-brother, on the expedition. She is instrumental in helping them and thus wins Roger's respect and affection.

45   Coleman, Lonnie. *Orphan Jim.* Doubleday, 1975.   (J, S)
       204p.

> My brother Jim was seven, and Mama had spoiled him. . . .

Trudy calls her brother Orphan Jim when she wants him to get a move on, or to rile him. The brother and sister go from one adventure to another as they survive the depression in Alabama.

46   Corcoran, Barbara. *A Dance to Still Music.* Illus. by   (J, S)
       Charles Robinson. Atheneum, 1974. 180p.

> At the end of the path, nestled in among the mangrove roots, was a small houseboat.

Unhappy over her loss of hearing and the prospect of attending a special school, teenager Margaret runs away from her new home in Key West, bound for her former home in Maine. She finds an injured Key deer fawn on the road and meets Josie, a kind lady who provides sanctuary on her houseboat. Here, through kindness and caring, Margaret comes to accept her handicap and look forward to a new future. Black-and-white drawings contribute to the authentic Florida Keys atmosphere.

47   Cormack, Maribelle. *Swamp Boy.* Illus. by Winfield   (I, J)
       Hoskins. McKay, 1948. 290p.

> The run was growing narrower and the drifts of Spanish moss completely cut off their view on either side.

Clint Sheppard spent much of his boyhood hunting and exploring in the Okefenokee swamp of Georgia, with Tom, a Seminole Indian, as companion. The focus of the story is on Clint's efforts to gain an education so that he can improve the conditions of his family. The details of the richness of the natural background will be of interest to the reader. The picture of the swamp is quite well-drawn.

48   Cotton, Nell. *Piney Woods.* Vanguard, 1962.   (I, J)
       160p.

> He crashed into Pa. Pa staggered, and the rifle went off with a terrible roar.

Running from his fears of the Florida wilderness in which he lives, Andy causes a near-tragedy, and earns the scorn of his big brothers, Mat and Joe. Wanting desperately to be a man and a valuable member of his pioneer family, he seems able only to disgrace himself. But, after an understanding neighbor teaches him to shoot and repair guns, Andy confronts a succession of crises, overcomes his fears, earns the respect and admiration of his family, and faces his future with new confidence.

49 Credle, Ellis. *Down, Down the Mountain.* Nelson,   (P)
      1932. unp.

> They each wanted a beautiful shining pair that sang "Creaky-squeaky-creaky-squeaky" every time they walked.

Attractively illustrated with brown and blue drawings by the author, this tale of little Hetty and her brother Hank gives a realistic picture of pioneer life in a log cabin in the Blue Ridge Mountains. Their wish for new shoes motivates them to plant, tend, and harvest their own field of turnips. Their experiences as they take their crop to market in the nearby village where a county fair is in progress provide the activities needed to make this an interesting tale.

50 Cummings, Betty Sue. *Let a River Be.* Atheneum,   (J, S)
      1978. 195p.

> She dreamed past her anger . . . seeing the tiny school of gray-green minnows darting, pausing, darting.

Ella Richards, an old, eccentric widow, lived in a dilapidated shack on the bank of the beautiful Indian River between Titusville and Cocoa, Florida. Angered by the ever increasing pollution and decay along the river, she devoted her energies and meager resources to a "save the river" fight. Joined, unexpectedly, by a retarded young man, who had been rejected by society, they made a team which had a real impact on the problem. Fine descriptive passages make the river the most important character in the story. Though the very earthy language used by Ella may offend the more sensitive reader, the ecological truths presented and the warm human feelings expressed far outweigh that aspect of the writing.

51 Davis, Burke. *The Summer Land.* Random, 1965.   (S)
      242p.

> The first priming . . . meant harvesting the lowest leaves on the tobacco stalks before they were scorched.

Fifteen-year old Fax (Fairfax) Starling is the hero-narrator of this tale of life on a North Carolina tobacco farm during the "tobacco wars" of 1916. Horse-trading; whiskey-making; coon-hunting; and feuding between white settlers, Indian halfbreeds, and their black neighbors are ways of life depicted in this funny, though often earthy, story of the growing-up of a teenage mountain boy. Educational opportunities, or lack of them, are pictured when an attractive, young school teacher, Miss Cassie, comes down from Virginia and takes over the local one-room school.

52   Davis, Harwell Goodwin. *The Legend of Landsee.*   (J)
     Strode, 1976. 268p.

> There was the imposing house known as Landsee Mansion which Aunt Mymee claimed was haunted and which stood vacant for many years.

This account of an Alabama community of a hundred years ago centers around the Landsee Mansion and the events which took place within its imposing walls. All the elements of despair, hope, and finally triumph which make an interesting story are found in this exciting tale of life as it was lived in another era.

53   Davis, Paxton. *The Seasons of Heroes: A Novel.*   (S)
     Morrow, 1967. 276p.   op

> We Gibboneys . . . have earned it thrice over for we have courted moonshine and misadventure. . . .

The three separate narratives of three generations of the Gibboneys of Virginia combine to form this novel. Matt, a career soldier, painfully chooses to accept a commission in the Confederate army in 1861; his son, Robert, accompanies Colonel McNaught on a disastrous mission into Pennsylvania in 1864; and, Robert's son, Will, in 1914 confronts a lynch mob and finds his chance for heroism. The story is united by the continuity of family, place, and the ideals of duty, honor, and country that each man embodies.

54   Dobler, Lavinia. *Glass House at Jamestown.* Illus.   (I, J)
     by John Jordan. Dodd, 1957. 126p.   op

> You know how to manage the kitchen . . . We have to eat. We need you where you are.

Young Nat Peckock expected such words but he was still unhappy. An orphan, one of the four boys at the Jamestown Colony, Nat disliked his kitchen job; more than that he wanted to become an apprentice glassblower with the Polish and German artisans who had been sent by the London Company to help the Jamestown colony become a profitable venture. By focusing on the economic, technical, and cultural aspects of the glassmakers in Jamestown, a unique view of the colony is presented.

55 Dykeman, Wilma. *The Tall Woman.* Holt, 1962. (S)
315p.

> . . . to help us find a way to live together, whether by law or knowledge or instinct or the love of God.

After the Civil War, Lydia McQueen and her family strive to remake their world. Old suspicions, hatreds, family quarrels, and personal desires for revenge created by that conflict must be resolved in order to restore peace, to rebuild their family ties, and to reunite the community. This absorbing narrative of rural life in the late 1800s follows Lydia's life as she marries Mark McQueen and they establish their family in the North Carolina mountains.

56 Edwards, Sally. *When the World's on Fire.* Illus. by (I, J)
Richard Lebenson. Coward, 1972. 125p.

> She was a victim of a bad dream, walking through a never-ending nightmare.

Annie, a nine-year-old slave girl, was living with her master, Timothy McGee, when the British occupied Charleston, South Carolina, in 1780. Her brother, Jack, was captured and taken to a British slave ship. Annie had to deliver kindling and clean the British barracks every day. Her master decided she was the only person who could set off an explosion to destroy the five thousand pounds of ammunition stored in the barracks. The conjurer woman, Maum Kate, encouraged Annie to take the risk for the sake of the black people in the community. Her attempts to carry out this daring act and her feelings of loneliness, fear, and helplessness are vividly portrayed in this book. Annie is a fictional character whose story is drawn from historical fact.

57 Ehle, John. *The Land Breakers.* Harper, 1964. (S)
407p.

> The sound of water had come to them to be the voice of the new land.

Searching for their own place in the wilderness, a group of settlers choose a North Carolina valley between Morganton and Watauga and try to conquer it. This story, which takes place during 1779–84, vividly portrays the settlers' struggles with wild animals, winter storms, and other hazards of nature as they attempt to tame a hostile land. The personal conflicts of these early mountain folk—their sorrows and their hopes, their humor and their strength—all are skillfully woven into an exciting, mature tale.

58 Farley, Walter. *The Black Stallion's Ghost.* Illus. (I, J, S)
by Angie Draper. Random, 1969. 187p.

It grew larger and began floating just above the saw grass, coming in his direction.

Alec Ramsay has brought the Black Stallion to a ranch on the edge of the Florida Everglades for a rest and vacation. During a casual ride into the glades, he finds himself inextricably involved with the strange and vaguely sinister circus performer, Captain Philip de Pluminel, and his incredibly well-trained gray mare. The captain's own fears, unique heritage, and ultimate fate lead Alec and the Black Stallion into a weird and terrifying encounter with a supernatural entity deep within the fastness of the swamp. Young readers should enjoy this sequel to the author's other Black Stallion stories which are now out-of-print.

59   Few, Mary Dodgen.   *Azilie of Bordeaux.*   Illus. by   (S)
Elizabeth Belser Fuller.   Carolina Editions, 1973.
335p.

The suffocating darkness seemed like a great animal about to spring. Azilie wanted to scream.

Escaping religious persecution in France in 1764, Azilie and the little band of Huguenots found life in provincial South Carolina full of hardships and danger. Only by her quick wit, courage, and independent spirit does Azilie survive and find romance in the New World. Youthful female readers will quickly identify with Azilie in her struggle for equality for women. Prominent historical figures in the novel include Patrick Calhoun, father of John C. Calhoun; Jean de la Howe; and Governor Thomas Boone.

60   Finney, Gertrude E.   *Muskets Along the*   (J, S)
Chickahominy.   Longmans, 1953.   242p.   op

How little the peninsula had changed . . . in the years since his father had sailed away for England.

Concealing his true identity, Andrew Foster Shields returns to Virginia as an indentured servant to the Constant family to reclaim the land Sir William Berkeley had taken from his parents. Before realizing his dream, Andrew becomes involved in Bacon's Rebellion. An insight into the social and political life of the Virginia colony is given in this interesting historical novel.

61   Fletcher, Inglis.   *Cormorant's Brood.*   Lippincott,   (S)
1959.   345p.

Anthony sighed with quiet elation . . . his adventure was getting off to an exciting start.

In 1663 England's Charles II granted a vast domain in America (now North Carolina) to eight noblemen who had helped him regain his

father's throne. These landlords, known as Lords Proprietors, governed
the territory under a constitution drawn up by John Locke. *Cormorant's
Brood* is the story of the colonists' struggle to gain justice and independence from the greedy, irresponsive governors who were sent to
rule them. Romance, intrigue, and excitement make this tale, based on
actual events, one which high school students will enjoy.

62   Fletcher, Inglis. *Lusty Wind for Carolina.* Berg,   **(S)**
         1973.   470p.

> Tar, pitch and turpentine, tobacco, hides; masts, timber, staves and
> shingles; port and tobacco. This was Carolina.

This exciting tale of one of the early colonial settlements along
the Cape Fear River centers around the struggle of Robert Fountaine,
a devout French Huguenot, as he attempts to find a place where he
and his family can enjoy religious freedom and rebuild his weaving
business. Harassment by pirates, attacks from unfriendly Indians, plus
the many difficulties of pioneer living encountered by the settlers
threaten the colony's success. However, the dedication of his daughter,
Gabrielle, and the assistance of many interesting friends bring the
story to a satisfying conclusion. The narrative contains enough romance
to interest girls and enough adventure to interest boys plus excellent
descriptions of the Cape Fear River area.

63   Fletcher, Inglis. *Raleigh's Eden.* Bobbs-Merrill,   **(S)**
         1940.   662p.

> Bronzed woodsmen stood shoulder to shoulder with unseasoned boys,
> giving them the strength of the far-flung forests, of the deep rivers.

This account of the revolutionary war and the "Iron Men of
Albemarle" has all the characteristics of an epic drama: action, intrigue,
strong characterization, and a love story. The most intense battles take
place not on a battlefield, but in the personal struggles of loyal English
subjects suddenly forced to choose between an unresponsive king and
the country they have come to love.

64   Fletcher, Inglis. *Rogue's Harbor.* Bobbs-Merrill,   **(S)**
         1964.   242p.

> Freedom! The most beautiful and significant word in the English
> language and the most important.

In 1677 the settlers of Perguimans' Precinct rebelled and struggled to keep the freedoms which were being denied them by the
Lords Proprietors, from whom they had obtained their much loved
land. The Willoughby family are the central figures in this novel of
colonial North Carolina. Their romances, adventures, and tribulations
provide the reader an exciting story.

65   Forbes, Tom H. *Quincey's Harvest.* Lippincott,   (J, S)
       1976. 143p.

I was surrounded by the living, the dying, and the dead—living things died so living things could live.

Quincey Evans was not a hunter at heart, but when rain washed out part of the tobacco crop, he knew he would have to help his father find food. Accustomed to the sharecropper's demanding way of life, Quincey must come to understand the ways of nature—why some creatures must die so others can live.

66   Forman, James. *Song of Jubilee.* Farrar, 1971.   (J)
       185p.

If you were free, Jim . . . if you were, where would you go?

Jim had been given to Myles McAdam as a Christmas present, so the Shenandoah Valley of Virginia was the only home he had ever known. Secretly taught to read by Myles's twin sister, Sharon, he was bitterly aware of his predicament as a slave; but when the outcome of the Civil War changed all that, he was forced to make the transition from slave to free man. Set in wartime, this first person narrative is richly and excitingly told.

67   Fox, John, Jr. *The Trail of the Lonesome Pine.*   (S)
       Grosset, 1908. 422p.   op

The big pine stood guard on high against the outer world.

John Hale, a young engineer, comes to the mountains to locate and mine the coal deposits there. He finds himself in the middle of a longtime feud between the Tollivers and the Falins, falls in love with June Tolliver, and after sending her off to be educated, loses his money but finally marries her. The novel has been made into a play.

68   Francis, Dorothy B. *Nurse of the Keys.* Avalon,   (I, J)
       1974. 191p.

"Now I can ask you to marry me. Will you, Lee? Will you?"

Nurse Lee Baxter accepts a private duty assignment caring for young Samantha, who has rheumatic fever. Romance blossoms between Lee and Samantha's acquaintance Pete Wheeler, driver of the Key West Conch Train, just as Lee's steady boy friend Kirk seems to be more and more involved with his charter boat job. An unexpected mystery puts Lee in danger as she realizes whom she really loves. Nursing is only incidental here, but the authentic Key West background helps make this a credible romance for young teens.

69   Francis, Dorothy B. *Run of the Sea Witch.* Illus.   (I, J)
by Monroe Eisenberg. Abingdon, 1978. 158p.

Big Mike brought the bow of the *Sea Witch* into the wind and cut
the engine.

Recently abandoned by his mother, twelve-year-old Donald has
to accompany his father, Big Mike; his older brother, Pepper; and his
grandfather, Kully, on a five-day run aboard the shrimp boat *Sea
Witch.* His development as he struggles to take his place in the opera-
tion of the family business and to understand the emotional problems
of the divided family makes a warm, engrossing story. Excellent descriptions of shrimp fishing and the struggles encountered in deep-sea
navigation add to the interest of the story. The artist's pen-and-ink
sketches give a realistic picture of various incidents in the narrative.

70   Gerson, Noel B. *Give Me Liberty: a Novel of Patrick*   (S)
Henry. Doubleday, 1966. 347p.   op

Tyrants have throughout all history been deaf to the demands of
free men for their liberties.

Patrick Henry was not afraid to speak for what he believed to be
the just and true rights of men. His oratory thrust him into the public
eye, and he became one of the strong voices for the Revolution in Virginia. Although his public career was an eventful and exciting one, he
eventually was forced to decline office in order to support his wife and
almost a score of children and grandchildren. Romance, history, and
examples of his oratory make this a colorful account of Patrick Henry's
life.

71   Gillett, Mary. *Bugles at the Border.* Blair, 1968.   (J, S)
220p.

He thinks us settlers are about the same as blackin' on his fancy
slippers.

Bart McLeod, orphaned grandson of Scottish McLeod, was
twelve years old in 1775 when Mecklenberg settlers declared their
freedom from England. Too young to fight when the war began in
earnest, he and his horse Donegal became important messengers for
the American forces in North Carolina. Throughout his adventures in
the war, Bart never forgot his hatred of his Tory schoolmate, Harry
Mowbray. His plot to capture Harry and thus avenge himself is an
exciting episode in this historical novel. Authentic background notes
are given in the foreword.

72   Glasgow, Ellen. *In This Our Life.* Harcourt, 1941.   (S)
467p.   op

You will find what you are looking for.

Asa Timberlake, a sixty-year-old impoverished aristocrat, worked in the stemming room of a tobacco house that once belonged to his grandfather. This is his story of the Timberlake family and their life in Richmond: Asa, his sickly wife, and their two daughters and their disastrous marriages. The author's concern for character development is evident.

73 Glasgow, Ellen. *Vein of Iron.* (Harcourt Modern (S)
Classics) Harcourt, 1950. 462p. (Paperback ed.,
Harcourt, 1967)

> Was the past broken off from the present? . . . or did that vein of iron hold all the generations together?

The Fincastle "iron vein of inner strength" has carried five generations of the family through good times and bad in the mountains of Virginia. The death of Grandmother Fincastle and the prosperity of World War I take the family to the city for a few prosperous years, but the poverty of the depression eventually leads them back to their old mountain home. Their strength of character helps them survive their struggles and attain happiness.

74 Griswold, Francis. *A Sea Island Lady.* Morrow, (S)
1939. 964p.

> It was a gala night for Charleston: everyone was there in finest feathers.

Emily, the Sea Island Lady, came to the area near Beaufort as the wife of a carpetbagger. She later married the son of a prominent South Carolina family. This well-researched novel tells the story of her family through several generations, from Reconstruction times to the 1920s. Descriptions of the war years and after, as well as life on the Sea Islands, is especially well done. The book has been likened to Margaret Mitchell's *Gone With the Wind.* There are maps on the endpapers.

75 Haas, Patricia Cecil. *Swampfire.* Illus. by Charles (I, J)
Robinson. Dodd, 1973. 187p.

> Fifteen yards in front of her . . . was the most beautiful horse that Sally had ever seen.

Almost every summer, Sally and her brother, Andrew, visited their cousin Anne on her peanut farm at the edge of the Dismal Swamp in Virginia. This year was special because Anne's child, Robin, promised to take them camping. The excitement increased when they learned that a ghost had been seen in the swamp. Robin had seen the ghost and thought that it was really a beautiful horse. They rescued the horse, escaped a swampfire, and solved the mystery of the swamp-ghost in this exciting story for teenagers.

76   Hall, Rubylea. *Davey.* Illus. by Ralph Ray, Jr.   (I, J)
Duell, 1951.   268p.   op

>   "Yessir," Davey replied, his eyes fixed on Pa's face, "but I done made eight grades. . . ."

Education was hard won for a tenant farmer's son in the backwoods of northern Florida during the 1920s, but for Davey it was all-important, and his Pa's decision that eight grades were enough was heartbreaking. Life on the farm was full of hard work and adventures, but Davey was eager to expand his horizons. In a thrilling climax he becomes a hero and earns the opportunity to stay in school. Strong characters, colorful and authentic settings, and plenty of action make this an effective story.

77   Hall, Rubylea.   *The Great Tide.*   Great American,   (S)
1975.   535p.

>   She stared, stupified by the massive elegance of the house. It towered two stories above her. . . .

Mrs. Carolina (Ca'line) Blackwell, seeking possessions and luxury, has married a wealthy and powerful man she does not love. The elegance, intrigue, and excitement she finds in her new home, the booming Gulf Coast city of St. Joseph, Florida, contrasts sharply with her girlhood at Greenwood Plantation. After the historic destruction of St. Joseph by disease and hurricane, Ca'line returns to Greenwood and true love. A colorful picture of life in antebellum west Florida is marred by an overly romantic style and stereotyped characters.

78   Hamilton, Betsy (pseud.).   *Southern Character*   (J, S)
Sketches.   Diety Press, 1937.   126p.

>   Betsy's girlhood was spent on this typical antebellum plantation, where she became familiar with the habits, characteristics and dialects of that period.

Born in Talladega County, Alabama, in 1843, Idora McClellan Moore captures in these sketches the real dialect of the northern Alabama hill country. The hill people and the plantation blacks of Alabama have never "had their stories told nor their lives painted so realistically and so sympathetically as in these sketches."

79   Hamilton, Elizabeth Verner.   *When Walls Are High.*   (I, J)
Illus. by Laura Peck.   Trodd Street Pr., 1973.   151p.

When walls are high, you can have some peace . . . you can get lonely, too.

Caroline and Felicia, when not in school, spend their time climbing the walls between the old houses and gardens in Charleston. In their attempt to discover a secret garden for themselves they meet and befriend an old man and his cats. As they work to clear his garden of rubbish, they begin to unravel his secret—a secret which eventually concerns Caroline's lawyer-father. A satisfying mystery for elementary grades with realistic family and peer relationships. A helpful map is on the endpapers.

80   Hamner, Earl, Jr.   *The Homecoming: a Novel about*   (J, S)
      Spencer's Mountain.   Random, 1970.   115p.

Let the whole world know that Clay Spencer was home.

It was Christmas Eve and Clay Spencer had failed to arrive home. While his children had faith that Santa Claus would come, their mother became discouraged as it grew later and later and her husband had not arrived. Clay-Boy, the oldest son, went to search for his father through the snow-covered Virginia mountains. The story ends happily when Clay Spencer does come home safely, bringing with him gifts for everyone. This is a companion volume to *Spencer's Mountain* and has been made into a television drama.

81   Hamner, Earl, Jr.   *Spencer's Mountain.*   Dial, 1961.   (J, S)
      247p.

It was a proud thing to be a Spencer man.

Clay Spencer was the proud father of eleven red-haired children. His oldest child, Clay-Boy, had a burning desire to get a college education, but his father thought it a waste of money. If Clay-Boy did go, he would be the first from New Dominion to leave his Blue Ridge home and the mountain to attend college. This is primarily a story about growing up and a family's love for one another and the land on which they have lived for generations. The television series, "The Waltons," was based on this book.

82   Haskins, Ida.   *Adventures on the Airboat Trail.*   (I, J)
      Illus. by Bob Lamme.   Seeman Publishing Co., 1973.
      141p.

The sun descended behind the cypress forest on the opposite side of the river and dusk settled in.

Brent and Rob, south Florida teenagers who grew up on the outskirts of the Everglades and are familiar with its dangers and challenges, take their visiting friend, Jim, on a camping/hunting trip aboard their airboat, the *Jolly Jolt*, into the deep reaches of this tropical wilderness. Vivid descriptions of the many different kinds of flora and fauna found in this untracked sea of grass are interspersed with exciting encounters with Indians, gunrunners, and the many dangers of the Everglades itself. Black-and-white line drawings add to the attractiveness of the book.

83   Hays, Wilma Pitchford.   *Mary's Star: a Tale of*   (I)
      Orphans in Virginia.   Illus. by Lawrence Beall Smith.
      Colonial Williamsburg, 1968.   108p.

   She thought that she had found she liked being a girl.

Mary Breckenridge wished very much that she was a boy. Often she dressed like one, acted like one, and rode like one. Mary, her older brother, and the apprentice Deke found themselvs alone and penniless in the world when Colonel Breckenridge was killed in the Revolution. As she tried to regain possession of her colt, Star, and as she realized that she must grow up and accept her new role in life, Mary found that being a girl can be useful. A clear and accurate picture is given of colonial laws and customs regarding the care of orphans in eighteenth-century Virginia.

84   Hays, Wilma Pitchford.   *The Scarlet Badge.*   Illus.   (I)
      by Peter Burchard.   Colonial Williamsburg, 1963.
      109p.

   His father's belief had brought heartache, defeat, and the loss of his home.

The "scarlet badge" was the red badge of loyalty to King George III worn by those who remained faithful to England. Loyalty to the crown was an unpopular cause in the midst of a people who supported the cause of revolution and rebellion. This is the story of Rob Roberts and his family who were forced to leave their home in Virginia and flee to England because of their beliefs.

85   Hays, Wilma Pitchford.   *Siege! The Story of St.*   (I, J)
      Augustine in 1702.   Illus. by Peter Cox.   Coward,
      1976.   94p.

   All the doomed houses were blazing now. Shots rang out. Men ran to and fro....

When English forces attack the Spanish settlement at Saint Augustine, Juan Alfonso with his mother and his sister seek protection within the stone walls of Castillo de San Marcos. Juan's family and the other residents withstand a seven-week siege, an ordeal which includes the burning of their homes. Young Juan's adventures during the siege contribute to an effective re-creation of a crucial period in the history of Spanish Florida. Authentic black-and-white illustrations bring out the flavor of life in America's oldest city.

86   Head, Ann.   *Mr. and Mrs. BoJo Jones.*   Putnam,   (S)
           1967.   253p.

   As the statistics say, most teen-agers who marry, marry because they have to.

BoJo and July had to. July was pregnant. They were both still in high school. Sick with shame, they married. Together they struggled towards maturity and the responsibility of parenthood. Both sets of parents seized the death of the premature baby as an opportunity to try to separate the couple, but instead BoJo decided to go to college and July went to work to support them. Miss Head, a South Carolina author, uses Beaufort for the setting of the story, changing the name to Trilby. It is a thoughtful and perceptive novel which puts the final solution in the hands of the two young adults. The growing love between BoJo and July becomes touching and believable. The appeal of the story is universal; and since the problems with which it deals are pertinent to modern family life, it could find a wide audience.

87   Heatter, Basil.   *"Wreck Ashore!"*   Farrar, 1969.   (J, S)
           154p.

   The wrecking schooners were already underway, standing out of the harbor under jibs and foresails. . . .

The salvaging of wrecked ships and their cargoes was a major industry in Key West, Florida, during the nineteenth century. When his uncle brings him to the Keys sometime after the Civil War, teen-aged Matt finds plenty of excitement and adventure, including a disastrous Seminole Indian attack. Loosely based upon historical events which actually occurred thirty to forty years earlier than this setting, the story offers plenty of action amidst the flavor of the sea and the Florida Keys.

88   Henry, Marguerite.   *Misty of Chincoteague.*   Illus.   (I)
           by Wesley Dennis.   Rand McNally, 1947.   172p.

   The air was wild with whinnies and snorts as the ponies touched the hard sand.

This story of the annual pony-penning at Chincoteague Island off the Virginia coast is essentially the story of Misty and the two children who owned her. As background, the first two chapters are devoted to the legend of the coming of the ponies to nearby Assateague Island from the wreck of a Spanish galleon before the days of colonial settlements in the New World. The atmosphere of the islands and an understanding of the freedom-loving ponies adds to the excitement and adventure. This story is followed by *Sea Star, Orphan of Chincoteague* and *Stormy, Misty's Foal*, both written by Mrs. Henry.

89   Henry, Marguerite.   *Sea Star, Orphan of*   (I)
         Chincoteague.   Illus. by Wesley Dennis.   Rand
         McNally, 1949.   172p.

> "Ain't he beautiful with that white star shining plumb in the center of his forehead."

In this sequel to *Misty of Chincoteague*, Paul and Maureen sell Misty to some movie people from New York to help send their uncle to college. They miss Misty greatly until they find an orphan colt on the beach and take him home. With the help of their grandparents and a mare who has lost her foal the children adopt the orphan colt. The realistic characters and picturesque background of the Eastern Shore add color and excitement to the story.

90   Henry, Marguerite.   *Stormy, Misty's Foal.*   Illus. by   (I)
         Wesley Dennis.   Rand McNally, 1963.   224p.

> "A mare colt, sound as a dollar."

Misty's foal was born after the great storm which almost destroyed Chincoteague Island and the herd of wild ponies on Assateague Island. After many adventures and with much concern for the safety of Misty, Maureen and Paul, aided by their grandparents, move Misty to the mainland to await the birth of her baby. Later, Misty and Stormy play an important role in helping raise money to rebuild the wild pony herd on the island. This is a sequel to *Misty of Chincoteague*.

91   Heyward, Dubose.   *Porgy.*   Illus. by Theodore   (S)
         Nadajen.   Scribner, 1925.   (Reprint ed., Berg, 1970)
         196p.

> No one remembered when he first made his appearance among the ranks of the local beggars.

Porgy, the crippled beggar, seemed doomed to a life of mediocrity until Bess comes along to share his home. Their lives take on an additional purpose when they acquire an infant whose parents have been lost in a hurricane. When Bess' former suitor returns to claim her, Porgy is transformed into a man of violence and, as a result, loses all that he holds dear. Full of emotion, humor, and pathos, the short novel portrays black life in Charleston during the 1920s.

92   Hoff, Syd.   *Irving and Me.*   Harper, 1967.   226p.   (I, J)

> There was a boy about my age on his knees, digging a hole in the sand.

The above quotation describes the way in which Artie, thirteen and slightly homesick for Brooklyn, meets Irving, his first and eventually his best friend, in his new hometown of Sunny Beach, Florida. From this meeting their adventures begin. Artie is recruited for the title role in *Julius Caesar* at the Community Center, meets a dream girl, learns to swim, becomes an entertainer, is beaten by the local bully and then reforms him, and learns to value both friendship and his own abilities. Entertaining and humorous light reading.

93   Holding, James.   *The Mystery of Dolphin Inlet.*   (J, S)
       Macmillan, 1968.   198p.

> Folks down our way like smoked mullet better than candy bars.

An exciting mystery, treasure hunters, scuba diving, and a bit of romance are interlaced with information about Florida's west coast Keys and their commercial fishing industry to make a novel which will appeal to readers of all ages. Pete Hobbs, a high school boy who works part-time at his father's fish market on Perdido Key, meets Susan Foster, an attractive Tallahassee teenager vacationing in the area, and the story begins to unfold. Information on the region's commercial and natural resources is accurate and interestingly given.

94   Holland, Marion.   *No Children, No Pets.*   Knopf,   (I)
       1956.   182p.

> Right outside there was a tall, curved coconut palm; one enormous frond hung down across the window.

Jane's mother inherits an apartment house in Florida. A trip to inspect the property turns into a permanent move for Jane, Don, Becky, Mother, and the cat, despite the previous owner's policy of excluding children and pets, and opposition from some of the tenants. Some minor mysteries and a hurricane add excitement. An old-fashioned children's book dated in style and portraying the Florida of thirty years ago, it is easy to read with typical family situations and humorous characters and incidents.

95   Hooker, Ruth, and Smith, Carole.   *The Pelican*   (P, I)
       Mystery.   Illus. by George Armstrong.   Whitman,
       1977.   128p.

> The house was built on stilts and had its own small dock.

One of the small Florida islands between Miami and Key West

on U. S. Highway 1 is the setting for this story of the adventures, mystery, and intrigue that a vacationing preteen brother and sister encounter as they spend several weeks in a small motel while their mother recuperates from a serious illness. Black-and-white drawings add realism to the author's descriptions of places, tropical birds, and animals.

96 Hunt, Irene. *The Lottery Rose.* Scribner, 1976. (J, S)
185p.

> "Maybe we're goin' to die, both of us," he whispered to the bush beside him.

Georgie, seven, physically abused in his slum home, has become withdrawn and antisocial. Sent by authorities to a children's home after a particularly severe beating, he takes along his only treasure, a bedraggled rosebush won in a raffle. A beautiful garden nearly becomes a new home for the bush. Through the garden's owner, Mrs. Harper, and her small retarded son, Robin, Georgie is finally able to know love and acceptance, both given and received. A moving story, simply and beautifully told.

97 Hurston, Zora Neale. *Jonah's Gourd Vine.* (S)
Lippincott, 1971. 316p.

> "Dey tole me tuh go find work, but Ah wish dey had uh tole me school...."

For sixteen-year-old John, son of an ex-slave, education was to be one of the stepping-stones to a new life as the Reverend Pearson, prominent Baptist clergyman of Orange County, Florida. Although a loving family man and the spiritual leader of the community, he is brought to his downfall by his own carnal impulses. Miss Hurston, a black anthropologist, weaves dialect, folklore, mores, and symbolism into this picture of southern black culture after the Reconstruction period and into the 1920s, while telling a story of Everyman's inner conflict with his own base nature.

98 Ironmonger, Ira. *Alligator Smiling in the Sawgrass.* (P, I)
Illus. by Sandra Davidson. Addison-Wesley, 1965. unp.

> In the very middle of this sawgrass swamp, the green alligator was switching his great tail.

The great alligator is smiling a greedy, toothy smile at each of the other swamp creatures: a turtle, a frog, and a purple gallinule. When drought parches the Everglades and the only water is that in the alligator's hole, these three come for a drink, but they must face that terrifying smile. Together, they trick the alligator, satisfy their thirst, and escape. A brief, simple story with a subtle moral and lavish, boldly colored illustrations.

99 Jarrell, Mary. *The Knee-baby.* Illus. by Symeon   (P)
Shimin. Farrar, 1973. unp.

> He remembered the slippery pine needles. . . .

North Carolina "folk-talk" has an important place in this simple picture book about a "knee-baby" (a little one-, two-, three-year-old), whose place on his mother's lap has been taken over by the newly born "lap-baby." As a result, Allan dreams of his "Mam-mommy" (grandmother), who always has a place for him on her lap. Colorful, sensitive pictures add to the warmth of the story. The author is the wife of the late Randall Jarrell and the story reflects the charm of their home in the Piedmont section of North Carolina.

100 Johnston, Mary. *To Have and To Hold.* Illus. by   (J, S)
F. C. Schoonover. Houghton, 1931. 331p.
(Paperback ed., Airmont, 1969)

> While the soul lives, love lives. . . .

A beautiful, young girl arrived with the cargo of brides sent from England to Virginia in 1621. Ralph Percy, a famous swordsman and one of the settlers, married her only to discover that she was a ward of the king and had fled England to escape Lord Carnal, a libertine nobleman and favorite of the king. Lord Carnal followed her to Virginia, and Ralph Percy was forced to defend his wife against the king's man. This romantic novel of early Virginia portrays the relationships of the colonists with the Indians, the British, and with each other.

101 Kane, Harnett T. *The Gallant Mrs. Stonewall: a*   (S)
Novel Based on the Lives of General and Mrs.
Stonewall Jackson. Doubleday, 1957. 320p.
(Reprint ed., Queen's House, 1976)

> Was Tom already dead? Had he and the cadets been wiped out by the marauders?

Anna Morrison Jackson was General Stonewall Jackson's second wife. Although their life together was brief due to Jackson's death from pneumonia after being wounded, their marriage was a deep and meaningful one. The account of the Civil War as it was seen and experienced by Mrs. Jackson is historically accurate. Visits with her husband during the war and the conversations among those actually involved in the struggle lend further credibility to her story.

102   Kane, Harnett T.   *The Lady of Arlington: A Novel*   (S)
      Based on the Life of Mrs. Robert E. Lee.   op
      Doubleday, 1953.   288p.

> I am a wanderer on the face of the earth.

Mary Curtis Lee must have often felt this way after defying her parents and marrying into the impoverished Lee family. Her courage, her tribulations as an army wife, the enforced separations from her adored husband, the loss of her beloved Arlington, and her struggle with ill health are narrated in a sympathetic account of her life from girlhood to the death of her husband. This biographical novel of Robert E. Lee's wife will increase interest in the great general himself.

103   Kane, Harnett T.   *The Smiling Rebel: a Novel Based*   (S)
      on the Life of Belle Boyd.   Doubleday, 1955.   314p.   op

> Let one of the Unionists try to stop her! Soon she ran alone . . . toward the army in gray.

An exciting social life in Washington came to an end for seventeen-year-old Belle Boyd in April, 1861, with the surrender of Fort Sumter. The family returned to their Martinsburg, Virginia, home. Like her father, Belle was determined to serve the Southern cause. She became a spy. Suffering imprisonment, abuse, discouragement, and exile, she returned from captivity to marry a Yankee officer. This story of intrigue and adventure during the Civil War is rich in the history of the Shenandoah Valley.

104   Knudson, R.R.   *You Are the Rain.*   Delacorte, 1974.   (J, S)
      unp.

> ". . . we're lost in a hurricane," I howl to June as we crawl for higher turf.

Eight teen-aged girls are on a camping trip in Everglades National Park when an out-of-season hurricane hits. Before the park rangers can evacuate the group, "Crash" Adams, the central character, and June Regan, the group misfit, are separated from the rest. Riding out the storm in the wilderness, they find new strengths and comradeship in the experience. Contemporary characters, authentic Everglades settings, and an unusually graphic description of the hurricane will make absorbing reading for teens despite a sometimes difficult style of writing.

105   Koch, Dorothy.   *Up the Big Mountain.*   Illus. by   (P)
      Lucy and John Hawkinson.   Holiday House, 1964.
      unp.

The sun is very hot, but we climb up, up, up. Then we come to a waterfall.

An easy-to-read story of a little girl and her brother, Joe, and their climb up the big mountain. The artistic, color illustrations add much to the simple text as the boy and girl admire the flowers, pick blackberries, and explore the many exciting aspects of mountain climbing. Though the "story" mountain could have been anywhere, the fact that the author lives and teaches in North Carolina gives it regional importance.

106 Konigsburg, E. L. *(George)*. Atheneum, 1970.   (I, J)
         (Paperback ed.,   Aladdin, 1974) 152p.

Only two people know that George was probably the funniest little man in the whole world. . . .

Those two people were Howard Carr and his older brother Benjamin, and they knew because George lived inside of Benjamin and spoke only to them. The surprising and sometimes hilarious events in the Carr's hometown of Lawton Beach, Florida, when Benjamin, who was in the sixth grade, brought George out are memorable. This whimsical touch of fantasy makes an appealing story about a very precocious small boy with an unusual way of finding solutions to typical and very contemporary problems.

107 Lancaster, Bruce. *Phantom Fortress*. Little, 1950.   (J, S)
         310p.

He's part rawhide and part vinegar, wrapped around the biggest heart on the continent.

These words were used to describe Francis Marion, the Swamp Fox. The story deals with Marion's campaign against the British Army in the Carolinas. Ross Pembroke, an officer from Rhode Island, serves under Marion and learns there is more than one way to wage a war. Dorande van Kortenaer, a French girl, serves as a secret agent for Marion's army. There are some vivid accounts of battles and burnings of homes in the story. An actual extract from a letter written to Marion by Nathanael Greene is included. The foreword gives factual information about the records used in writing the story.

108 Lancaster, Bruce. *Roll Shenandoah*. Little, 1956.   (S)
         316p.

The fuller stories in the *Tribune*, the *World*, and the *American* would quicken and deepen that hope.

In July, 1864, began a struggle which would give either the Northern or Southern forces the advantage in the Civil War. The

Union troops going into battle were dispirited but the appearance of a new leader revived their hopes. General Philip Sheridan rode into the scene. The events that followed are reported by a disabled Union officer, Ellery Starr, who, in his determination to see the Union cause to a victory, had signed as a war correspondent for the *New York Tribune*. His assignment was the Shenandoah Valley of Virginia. An action packed, romantic, and dramatic portrait of the people caught up in the war is presented in this historical novel.

109   Latham, Jean Lee. *The Story of Eli Whitney.*   Illus.   (I)
by Fritz Kredel.   Aladdin, 1953.   192p.   (Reprint   op
ed., Harper, 1962)

> I'm not raising Eli to be a mechanic.

Mr. Whitney wanted his first-born to graduate from Yale and be a teacher or a lawyer. Eli did graduate from Yale and headed for Georgia to become a tutor. Through the friendship of Mrs. Nathaniel Greene and Phineas Miller he went to Mulberry Grove on Cumberland Island to read law. While there he became interested in the problem of ginning cotton and in developing a machine to make growing upland cotton profitable. The book is interestingly written and gives an understanding of the struggles of a famous person.

110   Latham, Jean Lee. *This Dear-Bought Land.*   Illus.   (I, J)
by Jacob Landan.   Harper, 1957.   246p.

> We called it a free land, didn't we? It was not free. It was bought.

By a twist of fate, young David Warren comes to the New World in his father's place. The settlement of Jamestown and life in the colony as seen through David's eyes and his friendship with Captain John Smith make a lively adventure story. This work of historical fiction provides the reader with an understanding and appreciation of the struggles necessary to develop the first English colony and the roles of such leaders as Captain John Smith.

111   Lawrence, Isabelle. *Drumbeats in Williamsburg.*   (I)
Illus. by Manning de V. Lee.   Rand McNally, 1965.   op
224p.

> It's an order! In code! . . . If we had the code key we could figure it out.

Andy is sent to Williamsburg to stay with his cousins, the Budges, to keep him from joining Washington's army as a drummer boy. Williamsburg turns out to be anything but safe. Andy becomes involved with a Tory spy, meets Lafayette, and carries an important message to him, helps hide a runaway British drummer boy, and uses his uniform to go behind British lines. Finally he becomes a drummer for Lafayette and participates in the Battle of Yorktown. This action packed adventure story is filled with details about colonial life.

112   Lawrence, Isabelle. *A Spy in Williamsburg.* Illus.   (I)
       by Manning de V. Lee. Rand McNally, 1955. 224p.
       (Paperback ed., Rand McNally)

       Perhaps the spy seeks Henry's secret list.

When the young apprentice, Giles, moves into Ben's family's home in Williamsburg strange things begin to happen. Ben captures the British spy and helps Patrick Henry save the colonial capital from the enemy. The suspense makes this an exciting story of the time before the Revolution.

113   Lawrence, Mildred. *One Hundred White Horses.*   (I, J)
       Illus. by Oscar Liebman. Harcourt, 1953. 176p.

       If you counted a hundred white horses you got your wish, whatever it might be.

Eleven-year-old Penny Page needs twenty-three more white horses to make one hundred. But white horses are scarce in the wilderness country along Florida's Indian River in 1886, where her family has come to open a store at Mockingbird Cove. Not only that, but competition from the trading boat which plies the river threatens the success of her father's business. How Penny schemes to help her father, finds her one hundred white horses, and gets her wish make a readable and engaging story.

114   Lawrence, Mildred. *Sand in Her Shoes.* Illus. by   (P, I)
       Madge Lee Chastain. Harcourt, 1949. 211p.

       When you really get sand in your shoes, you'll never want to live anywhere but Florida, he told her.

Ten-year-old Dorrit and her older brother, Sandy, move to a small east-coast Florida town when their father takes over the weekly newspaper, the *Clarion*. The story of their adventures as they learn to know and love this typical tourist community include vivid descriptions of an ocean-side town of the 1930s, warm family relationships, a slight mystery, and even a real hurricane. Episodes set in the *Clarion*'s small printing plant provide an excellent picture of the linotype machine and "big" press on which small newspapers were printed back in those times. Black-and-white line drawings add depth and understanding to the text.

115 Lay, Elery. *Trek to the King's Mountain.* Moore,   (S)
1976. 195p.

> On finishing the meal, Shelby took the spy to Campbell. Tom went along with his book.

Haunted by the traumatic memory of the murder of his family by Indians, Tom Lea joins the "overmountain volunteers" in an attempt to conquer his panic in times of danger. Determined to prove his worth to his sweetheart, Patsy Dee, he finds security in his appointment as scribe to Colonel Shelby. Boys especially will enjoy the vivid portrayal of wartime activities and battle events as Tom and his comrades push on to King's Mountain and their successful defeat of Colonel Patrick Ferguson.

116 Lee, Harper. *To Kill a Mockingbird.* Lippincott,   (J, S)
1960. 296p.

> Miss Caroline was no more than twenty-one . . . She looked and smelled like a peppermint drop.

A story about conscience—how it is instilled in two children, Scout and Jem Finch; how it operated in their father, Atticus, a lawyer appointed to defend a black on a rape charge; and how it grows in their small Alabama town. The appealing plot, amusing incidents, and crisp style make it a most readable novel.

117 Lee, Mildred. *Honor Sands.* Lothrop, 1966. 225p.   (J, S)

> All about lay the little town of Cypress. She had lived here all her life. . . .

Honor is fourteen, experiencing the pangs and pleasures of adolescence. She wonders how to attract and deal with boys, envying her best friend who has no trouble doing either. Her life centers around her close-knit family and her friends and has few real crises. Then in the summer before tenth grade, she notices her father's attentions toward her beautiful unmarried aunt, and begins to fear a possible breakup of her family. However, a happy ending brings romance all around.

118 Lee, Mildred. *The Rock and the Willow.* Lothrop,   (I, J)
1963. 223p.

> "You never saw any fox, Leeroy," Enie said, patiently. "I don't believe there's any foxes around Tired Creek at all."

To any person born in Alabama, especially the southwestern part from Montgomery to Mobile, the characters of Earline (Enie) Singleton and her family of poor farmers are a reality. Earlene pursues a dream that someday she will see the world; someday she will go to college. The interest of an English teacher nurtures that dream and, despite family deaths and teenage problems, Enie keeps true to her hope.

119 Lee, S. C. *Little League Leader.* Illus. Strode, (I, J)
1974. 143p.

> In sports he would attempt to be the best in whatever position a coach placed him.

Huntsville, Alabama, and its many interesting environs come to life in this story of Paul, who moved there with his family during his preteen years. His adventures playing with the Little League team there provide an interesting and exciting story which will appeal especially to young boys.

120 Lenski, Lois. *Blue Ridge Billy.* Lippincott, 1946. (I)
203p.

> Hit's just a quiet little tune-box, just for soft, lonesome little tunes you play at home by yourself.

Set in Ashe County, North Carolina, this story of Billy Honeycutt, an appealing ten-year-old boy, gives a realistic picture of life on a farm in a remote area of the Blue Ridge Mountains in earlier times. Native crafts such as herb (yarb) gathering, split oak basketry, and grist mill corn grinding are cleverly woven into the background of Billy's struggle to understand his father's reluctance to allow him to develop his talent for "fiddlin'." A comprehensive list of mountain words and phrases will aid the reader in coping with the dialect used in conversations. The foreword gives one a background for the author's interest in and study of regional literature. Mrs. Lenski's delightful line drawings add depth to the reader's understanding of mountain life in those long ago times.

121 Lenski, Lois. *Peanuts for Billy Ben.* (Roundabout (P, I)
American Series) Lippincott, 1952. 128p.

> "We all got to chop. Chop all day—if we want a big crop!"

Six-year-old Billy Ben lived with his family on a sharecropping farm in the peanut growing region of Virginia. From planting to harvesting, peanut farming was long and hard work. The story relates the life of Billy Ben and the good times and hardships of a family working together during a one-year cycle of the peanut crop. The book also contains simple poetry relating to peanut growing. The author's pen and ink sketches add to the realism of the text.

122   Lenski, Lois.   *Strawberry Girl.*   Lippincott, 1945.   (I, J)
194p.

"We seen enough of your fine fixin's. Guess we know now how biggety you folks is. . . ."

Ten-year-old Birdie Boyer and her family have come to central Florida to start a strawberry farm. But their neighbors, the Slaters, who seem to lack the Boyers' ambition, resent their fences and their simple comforts, and conflicts grow between the two families. Through it all, Birdie yearns to go to school and to learn to make music. Her wishes finally come true in this colorful story of life during the early 1900s when old Florida Cracker ways were changing to newer lifestyles.

123   Lippincott, Joseph Wharton.   *The Phantom Deer.*   (I, J)
Illus. by Paul Bransom.   Lippincott, 1954.   192p.

There were plenty of deer on Big Pine Key, the miniature Key Deer. . . .

Old man Hickey, regarded as a hermit, lives on Big Pine Key and, in the time before Florida's Key Deer were a protected species, does his best to keep them from being exterminated by poachers. He and his great-nephew, Jack, rear an orphan fawn, who grows up to be the most magnificent of the Key Deer bucks, the one most sought by Finney, the poacher. The continuing pursuit of the deer and the conflict between Hickey and Finney make this an action-packed nature story.

124   Lippincott, Joseph Wharton.   *The Wahoo Bobcat.*   (I, J)
Illus. by Paul Bransom.   Lippincott, 1950.   207p.

The Tiger's spirits soared. He pranced and dashed in circles around his mate. . . .

The king of the Wahoo water prairie of central Florida is the magnificent bobcat known as the Tiger, threatened only by man with his dogs, guns, and encroaching civilization. Despite this, the Tiger forms an unusual friendship with the boy Sammy. Their friendship provides a focal point for this extraordinary nature story, but its theme is the life of the wild creatures great and small in the rapidly disappearing Florida wilderness. The impact of man and his improvements is made a natural part of the story.

125   Ludman, Barbara.   *The Strays.*   Nelson, 1976.   149p.   (J, S)

The stranger sprawled in the gutter, dazed. She was the palest sight I'd ever seen.

Mary Frances Allen and her family are used to taking in stray dogs. Now it is people like Stella Shanks and her "no-account" family who have moved into the sleepy south Florida town of Monroe. Involvement with the newcomers leads Mary Frances and her friends into a confrontation with the law and a reappraisal of community values. This warm and pleasant junior novel of small-town life and youthful innocence manages to be convincingly realistic but neither ugly nor harsh.

126 McNeer, May. *Bloomsday for Maggie.* Illus. by   (J, S)
Lynd Ward. Houghton, 1976. 246p.

> Mama shrieked, "Magnolia Murphy, are you out of your mind? Oh, Magnolia," she wailed. . . .

Maggie, awkward, eighteen, and a recent high school graduate, wants to be a newspaper reporter, but in Baghdad, Florida, in 1925, journalism was a man's world. She lands a job with the Baghdad *Trumpet* as an unpaid assistant to the Society Editor but longs to write for the front page. Maggie's humorous adventures and misadventures on the way to realizing her ambition shake up both the paper and the community. The flavor of boom-time Florida comes through in this story of a young woman determined to be liberated.

127 MacNeill, Ben Dixon. *Sand Roots.* Blair, 1963.   (S)
444p.

> What was then the fanciful dream of girlhood was now the reality that encircled her.

Born in the shadow of Hatteras Light into one of the old seagoing families of the Outer Banks, Danny Gray struggles to resolve his inner conflict between the island's traditions and a more modern life-style. Danny's story, set at the end of World War II, is an exciting one—spiced with romance, family relationships, sea-rescue operations, and a bit of mystery. Traditions of the islands' surfmen, now members of the Coast Guard, are skillfully woven into this well-written, descriptive novel of life on Hatteras Island. MacNeill's more scholarly work, *The Hatterasman*, a chronicle of four hundred years of the island's history, would probably appeal to the more mature reader.

128 Maddox, Hugh. *Billy Boll Weevil.* Illus. Strode,   (P)
1976. unp.

> This book is about the Boll Weevil Monument, which is located in Enterprise, Alabama.

This story of the "pest who becomes a hero" not only entertains young readers, but it also tells of the only monument in the world that is known to glorify a pest. This was the means which the citizens of Enterprise, Alabama, and Coffee County used to show their thanks for the part which the boll weevil played in causing farmers to diversify the economy and abolish one-crop agriculture.

129   Mason, David P.   *Five Dollars a Scalp: The Last*   (J)
      Mighty War Whoop of the Creek Indians.   Illus.
      Strode, 1975.   202p.

     The Fort Mims Massacre was tragic for our Alabama Indians.

This is perhaps the most valuable book that has ever been written about the Indians in Alabama. The author is part Indian. He shows both sides of the conflicts between the white men and the Indian.

130   Meader, Stephen W.   *Phantom of the Blockade.*   (J, S)
      Harcourt, 1962.   190p.

     The next cordon of gunboats must be right ahead, and Anse peered harder than ever into the wet, stormy blackness.

When Union gunboats destroy his stranded sloop, Anse turns from trading along the Outer Banks to running the Union blockade. As a crewman and eventually a pilot, Anse learns the tricks used by the runners who carry cotton to the Bahamas in exchange for guns, ammunition, and other supplies bound for Confederate troops.

131   Means, Florence Crannell.   *Shuttered Windows.*   (J, S)
      Houghton, 1938.   205p.

     Granny, why do you kneel facing East when you pray? And why do you bow three times . . . ?

Harriet, a young black girl from the North, comes to the Sea Islands of South Carolina to live with her great-grandmother. Here she finds a world entirely different from her earlier experiences in other places. When the choice about her future is to be made, Harriet decides to remain in the South among her people. The book gives a realistic picture of school life for black children in South Carolina, and will be helpful in building ancestral pride.

132   Messer, Ronald K.   *Shumway.*   Nelson, 1975.   190p.   (I, J)

     Ain't a white boy in Mount Holly will . . . have nothing to do with you after this.

Shumway, a white boy growing up in a small town in South Carolina in the turbulent 1950s, finds his easygoing life suddenly disrupted and his friendship with Lyle, a black boy, threatened as racial tensions mount one hot summer. With ethics all his own Shumway shares a dangerous secret with Lyle until the story reaches an explosive climax one night when Ku Klux Klan members get drunk. Shumway gains new insight into a white friend Dennis and about himself as he faces a changing way of life.

133 Milton, Hilary. *November's Wheel.* Abelard-   (I, J)
Schuman, 1976. 186p.

> Boy! . . . Boy howdy! never saw a prettier one.

The shiny green bicycle in the window of Wright's Market, in a little Alabama town, was to be raffled off next Saturday. The story of Billy Bob's decision to work for Mr. Wright—to trade work for raffle tickets is a heartwarming one. During that bleak November week, Billy Bob grows up. What he earns for his efforts is a surprise for the reader.

134 Mitchell, Margaret. *Gone with the Wind.*   (J, S)
Macmillan, 1936. 1,037p.

> If I have to steal or kill—as God is my witness, I'm never going to be hungry again.

The above quotation aptly expresses Scarlett O'Hara's determination and explains her drive for wealth. Through the story of Scarlett, her family, and friends, the author tells the story of Atlanta, the South, and the Civil War. It is filled with drama and excitement. The detail is realistic and true to the South as it was immediately preceding, during, and after the war. This well-known novel represents what happens to individuals any time a society falls apart for whatever reason.

135 Murphy, Robert. *The Pond.* Illus. by Teco   (J, S)
Slagboom. Dutton, 1964. 254p.

> They sat . . . savoring the thought that all this, and the Pond . . . were theirs for three days. . . .

In 1917 Joey and his friend Bud travel the muddy roads from Richmond to the Pond in a Model T to hunt and fish. This is a retelling of the adventures of fourteen-year-old Joey during his visit to the Pond and his stay with Mr. Ben, the caretaker. Through his association with the Pond; its wildlife and woods; Mr. Ben and Sam White's dog, Charley, Joey learns to understand wildlife. The delicate balance between boyhood and manhood is simply but accurately described.

136 Oertel, Theodore E. *Jack Sutherland: a Tale of*   (J, S)
Bloody Marsh. Crowell, 1926. 325p. (Reprint ed.,   op
Reprint Co., 1974)

44

My father was a soldier and his son must not prove a coward.

The central character, purely fictional, stows away on the first boat load of colonists to Georgia, develops along heroic lines as an indispensable aide to General Oglethorpe, and is present at the famous Battle of Bloody Marsh—part of the military struggle against the Spanish settlements in the South. The novel presents a good picture of conditions in Georgia's colonial era, as well as the historical background of many present-day tourist attractions in the coastal area.

137 Olsen, Theodore. *There Was a Season.* Doubleday, (S)
1972. 444p.

The first and perhaps primary reason for the change in Davis was the death of his bride. . . .

The early life of Jefferson Davis, president of the Confederacy, not only is interesting reading but perhaps explains some of Davis's later characteristics. As a West Point graduate he is regarded as one of the most promising students, well-liked for his wit, love of sports, and good humor. While stationed in Wisconsin he falls in love with pretty, spirited Sarah Knox Taylor, daughter of Zachary Taylor, his commanding officer. The ordeals of their courtship and the tragedy of their marriage make an engaging story.

138 Owen, Guy. *Journey for Joedel.* Crown, 1970. (S)
189p.

. . . It is their life's blood, these thin leaves of tobacco which the family lifts, holds, and passes now.

Joedel has accompanied his father to the tobacco auction before, but this will be the first time he has a basket of tobacco to sell. It is a gift from the landowner for whom his family sharecrops, damaged leaves which he has doctored up in hopes it will pass the scrutiny of the buyers. Joedel's proud, ambitious father; his hard-working, Indian mother; sharecroppers; landowners; "pinhookers" who speculate on tobacco prices; and tobacco farmers, white and black—good and evil—are skillfully brought to life in this story of rural life near the Cape Fear River during "Roosevelt times."

139 Page, Elizabeth. *The Tree of Liberty.* Holt, 1939. (S)
958p.

The mountains seen in sunlight were magical in their October coloring. . . .

Matthew Howard, frontiersman, meets Jane Peyton, a Tidewater aristocrat. They fall in love, marry, and work together to build a home and raise a family in the new frontier in the valley beyond the Blue Ridge. Jane, sympathizing with the social and political views of the aristocrats, and Matthew, sympathizing with the views of the frontiersmen, have conflicts parallel to those in the history of Virginia and the new nation. Through three generations of the Howard family, a marriage and a young nation grow into a strong union. Jefferson, Hamilton, and other leaders figure prominently in the story.

140 Page, Thomas Nelson. *Two Little Confederates.*   (I, J)
Illus. by John W. Thomason. Scribner, 1932. 190p.   op

It seemed to the boys that to be a soldier was the noblest thing on earth.

This lively adventure story of two small boys living on a Virginia plantation during the Civil War is based on the author's boyhood recollections. A realistic, but often amusing, picture of family life beset by the ravages of war is presented. Its authentic dialect enhances its character presentations.

141 Petersham, Maud, and Petersham, Miska. *The Silver*   (P, I)
Mace; a Story of Williamsburg. Illus. by Maud and
Miska Petersham. Macmillan, 1956. 38p.

Williamsburg soon became the heart and center of Virginia life as well as the seat of government.

This book clearly and simply tells of the first permanent settlement at Jamestown and the beginning of the colony at Williamsburg. It gives an interesting picture of life in the colonial capitol of Virginia from its time as the center of government to its restoration.

142 Pierce, Ovid Williams. *On a Lonesome Porch.*   (S)
Doubleday, 1960. 260p.

Brick walks, like steel spokes, led from a stone birdbath to the ivy bed.

Post-Civil War days on the Gray plantation, near Warren, North Carolina, are vividly portrayed in this fictionalized account of the return of Miss Ellen, her widowed daughter-in-law Lucy, and her grandson Garrett to their beloved home on the Moratuck River. Teenagers may be deterred by the emphasis given to resolving Miss Ellen's attempt to cope with the new pattern of life she finds being forced upon her. However, the vivid descriptions of the countryside and the sympathetic portrayal of the problems posed by the loss of loved ones, material possessions, and personal security make this an imaginative re-creation of a long ago period of history.

143 Powell, Richard. *I Take This Land.* Scribner,   **(S)**
1962. 437p.

> Ward Campion rode upriver along the cattle trail, squirming this way and that in the saddle.

Campion had come to Fort Taylor, Florida, just in time to play a major role in the area's development. This sweeping, well-written novel details his life, loves, and fortunes from 1895 to 1954, while presenting an authentic picture of the taming of the southwest Florida wilderness. Actual historical events and personalities are incorporated into the story, although the author takes some liberties with their time and place. Its length and a few detailed but relevant love scenes make this a book for mature readers.

144 Prather, Ray. *Anthony and Sabrina.* Macmillan,   **(P)**
1973. unp.

> I'll race you to the tree. Last one there is a muddy pig.

Typical brother-sister bickering and teasing between Sabrina and her older brother, Anthony, enliven this simple story of a young black mother as she takes her youngsters to visit "Big Ma's" farm in northwest Florida. The author's black pencil-and-wash drawings with overlays of yellow and brown add to the realistic picture of rural north Florida countryside.

145 Pratt, Theodore. *The Barefoot Mailman.* Duell,   **(S)**
1943. 215p.

> Steven walked a shimmering ribbon of heat waves, so strong that they often created a mirage on the sand. . . .

During the 1880s, before Flagler's railroad civilized Florida's Gold Coast, mail between Palm Beach and Miami was carried on foot along the beach, a three-day trip each way. This unusual service is the basis for the story of young Steven Pierton, a mailman, and his courtship of the lovely Adie, in competition with the wily promoter Sylvanus Hurley. A historically authentic setting, colorful characters, romance, and adventure combine to make entertaining reading.

146 Pratt, Theodore. *The Big Bubble.* Duell, 1951.   **(S)**
230p.

> "Listen, Eve, this is the damndest place ever for what I want to do."

Adam Paine, brilliant young architect, brings his wife, Eve, to Florida in late 1917. Together, they become part of the great Florida real estate boom, with Adam designing and building lavish estates and

Eve creating their furnishings. With success comes trouble, as the seductive and brazen Mona Otis entices Adam away from Eve, and the promoter Gerry Vance encourages Adam's extravagant ventures which prove to be disastrous when the bubble breaks. However they are finally reunited in a happy ending to this colorful story for mature readers.

147   Price, Eugenia.   *Beloved Invader.*   Lippincott, 1964.   (S)
      284p.

> The impact of this moment on Frederica Road pushed out the walls of his soul. . . .

Christ Church assists Anson Dodge in his efforts first to find himself and then to establish rapport with the Saint Simons Island inhabitants who are recovering from the ravages of the Civil War. Anson's efforts to give totally of himself to his beloved islanders is sustained by the love of two women—the vivacious Ellen, and Anna Gould, a plain woman with an indomitable character. This is the third in the trilogy about Saint Simons Island, Georgia, all of which are based on factual material.

148   Price, Eugenia.   *Don Juan McQueen.*   Lippincott,   (J, S)
      1974.   384p.

> A gentleman of honor goes on, with courage, with strength; never burdening his family or friends with his troubles.

Forced to leave his beloved family and home in Georgia to escape debtor's prison, John McQueen (loyal patriot and friend of General Washington, Jefferson, and Lafayette) fled to Saint Augustine where he transferred his loyalty to the Spanish king and became an advisor to east Florida's Governor, Quesada. Based on documented incidents the story presents a vivid picture of Spanish/British border struggles and Indian attacks, as well as the day-to-day hardships endured by colonists both Spanish and British in the post-Revolutionary era. The author's afterword gives additional information about her sources of research and the current location of some of the story's sites.

149   Price, Eugenia.   *Lighthouse.*   Lippincott, 1971.   (S)
      342p.

> We mortals are created so as to dream dreams. My dream has always been. . . .

In James Gould's case, the dream was to build a lighthouse. He found the chance to do so on Saint Simons Island, Georgia. This novel, the earliest chronologically in the Saint Simons trilogy, pursues the his-

tory of the Gould and Bunch families and centers on the career of
James Gould, Yankee-come-South, in the first decades of the nineteenth
century. The story follows Gould's fortunes from his restlessness as a
proud, novice builder, who hates slavery and grieves for a lost love up
North, to an adventurous lumberman and contractor, who winds up
with a loving wife, children, and ownership of several blacks.

150   Price, Eugenia.   *Maria.*   Lippincott, 1977.   352p.   (S)

> Dry, dusty, quaint St. Augustine was her city now. She was going to
> like and conquer it.

Saint Augustine, 1763, recently wrested by the British from the
Spanish, is the locale for this exciting story of Maria Evans, a beautiful
English midwife-nurse who comes here via Havana with her soldier-
husband. Difficult Spanish/British relationships, struggles of the loyalist colony during Revolutionary times, and the trauma of being traded
back to Spain are described as the background for Maria's various experiences. The author's afterword gives the historical facts on which
the story is based, pinpointing actual places in restored Saint Augustine which appear in the narrative.

151   Price, Eugenia.   *New Moon Rising.*   Lippincott,   (S)
        1969.   281p.

> A man does have a choice . . . he can choose despair or . . . faith.

The second novel in the Saint Simons Island trilogy continues the
story of the Gould and Bunch families. This one is centered around
Horace Bunch Gould, son of James, and how he makes his choices and
the consequences of these on him and his family. The novel covers the
period immediately before and during the Civil War. Some of the
places described still stand on this island paradise just off the coast of
south Georgia. Also, the graves of the people in the story can be visited
at the Christ Church cemetery.

152   Pyrnelle, Louise-Clarke.   *Diddie, Dumps and Tot: or*   (I, J)
        Plantation Child-Life.   Anne Mudd Cabaniss
        (reissued, Pelican, 1963).   105p.

> ". . . How silly you do talk, Dumps!" said Diddie. "There ain't any
> Injuns between here and New Orleans."

Diddie, Dumps, and Tot are the love-names given to three little
sisters who lived a plantation childhood in the 1800s, prior to the Civil
War. Legends, traditions, stories, games, and customs of the times delight the reader; but along with the laughter is sober moral teaching.
For the upper primary grades, this is good read-aloud material.

153 Rawlings, Marjorie Kinnan. *The Secret River.*   (P, I, J, S)
Illus. by Leonard Weisgard. Scribner, 1955. unp.

> She heard a sound like music. The forest had ended. Calpurnia has found the secret river.

A magical place where a child's dreams come true: this is the secret river. Her father has no fish to sell in his market, so the little girl, Calpurnia, and her dog, Buggy-Horse, have sought and found the secret river where there are many fish to catch. After magical adventures, Calpurnia brings home enough fish for the whole community, and hard times go away. Brief, poetically written (Calpurnia often speaks in poetic form), and dramatically illustrated, this is the author's only story written for young children.

154 Rawlings, Marjorie Kinnan. *The Yearling.* Illus.   (I, J, S)
by N. C. Wyeth. Scribner, 1967. 405p.

> Beyond the sinkhole, past the magnolia, under the liveoaks, a boy and a yearling ran side by side. . . .

Life on an isolated Florida farm is lonely for young Jody until the fawn, Flag, becomes part of it. As the lad shares in the triumphs and trials of his family's pioneer life, he doesn't realize the conflicts his pet will cause. With the inevitable heartbreak in the loss of Flag, he finds new understanding and begins to leave boyhood behind. The novel is unsurpassed in its portrayal of the central Florida wilderness, its strong and vivid characterizations, dramatic story elements, and sheer beauty of style.

155 Roberts, Nancy. *Sense of Discovery: the Mountain.*   (P, I)
Photographs by Bruce Roberts. John Knox Pr., 1969.
90p.

> "Follow my trail, follow my trail," she heard a voice say in a slithery, whispery way.

On a visit to the mountains, Nancy Lee goes off alone and discovers a cave which leads her to a new part of "her" mountain. She meets Ivey, a man dressed in buckskins and coonskin cap, and with him as guide explores the mountain's many wonders. Nancy Lee encounters both the friendly and beautiful, the cruel and dangerous, and sees the seasons change as if by magic. Both she and Ivey are sad when the time comes to go home, but she will keep the mountain's secret as her very own treasure. The excellent photography and informative text will excite the curiosity of children just discovering the world of nature, and will serve as a springboard for further learning—both independently and in the classroom.

156   Rockwood, Joyce.   *Long Man's Song.*   Holt, 1975.   (I, J)
207p.

I'll conjure there against our enemy until I've won this battle and turned the curse back upon the sender.

These are the words of Soaring Hawk, a young Cherokee Indian living in the southern Appalachian Mountains before the coming of the white man. According to the well-known anthropologist who wrote the foreword, the story is "ethnologically accurate and the facts are woven into the plot as integral elements." Two of the tales told as a part of the story are adapted from ancient Cherokee tales.

157   Rosenberger, Francis Coleman, ed.   *Virginia Reader:*   (J, S)
A Treasury of Writings from the First Voyage to the
Present.   Dutton, 1948.   576p.   (Reprint ed.,
Octagon, 1971)

. . . I have ranged through the rich and varied writing of Virginia. . . .

Through selections from more than sixty authors, arranged chronologically by the date of the author's birth, the editor introduces the reader to Virginia history and literature. Most of the authors were born in Virginia or lived for a substantial period in Virginia, and a short biography of each is included. Collected in one volume are narratives, journals, letters, poems, state papers, public addresses, essays, sketches, short stories, and excerpts from novels, each selected to tell the story of Virginia. It is useful as a reference and source of the more important works of writers of the different periods of Virginia history and as a sampling of various forms of literature. A brief annotation for each work is included with the text; and although there is an index to authors, a fuller index would be helpful.

158   St. John, Wylly Folk.   *The Christmas Tree Mystery.*   (I)
Illus. by George Porter.   Viking, 1969.   141p.

Trace even acted mad, most of the time, at his own father. . . .

Trace and baby Pip are the step-brother and step-sister of the central characters, Maggie and Beth. Several days before Christmas the ornaments are stolen from the tree in their home. Beth, as she is prone to do, jumps to a conclusion based on scant evidence, and accuses Pete. Trace convinces the girls it could not have been Pete so they set out to solve the mystery and clear Pete. The other queer happenings, the clues, how the girls discover the ornament-grabber and at the same time solve why Trace is so difficult, make an interesting and satisfying mystery story. The book describes the typical family and community activities of a small Georgia town at holiday time.

159 St. John, Wylly Folk. *The Ghost Next Door.* Illus.   **(I)**
by Trina Schart Hyman. Harper, 1971. 178p.

> Oh, she knew where it was . . . She used to live here.

Thus Sherry talks about her imaginary playmate named Miranda, who tells her things only the real Miranda and her aunt, Miss Judith, could have known. But Miranda drowned years ago, a fact her father never told his second wife and daughter. After many years, they visit Miss Judith who notices that the child, Sherry, bears an uncanny resemblance to Miranda. Convinced that Sherry is in touch with the spirit world, her aunt consults a famous medium for advice. The outcome is surprising and leaves the reader to draw his own conclusion.

160 St. John, Wylly Folk. *The Secret of the Seven Crows.*   **(I)**
Illus. by Judith Gwyn Brown. Viking, 1973. 188p.

> If we do come here tomorrow to stay, it'll be the scariest place we ever lived.

Shelly's father is allowed to rent the abandoned old house; but the owner will not sell it for a school until Gale, his daughter, finds a treasure left her by an eccentric old lady. The poltergeists who harass the new tenants turn out to be kids paid by drug smugglers protecting their stash. After this, Shelly helps track down the seven crows, and Gale gets her treasure. The kids, with Gale's crow, Dracula, and brother Jason's gourmet cooking and maddening competence are fun to know and the mystery is intriguing.

161 St. John, Wylly Folk. *The Secrets of the Pirate Inn.*   **(I)**
Illus. by Frank Aloise. Viking, 1968. 212p.

> They were all in the family room that morning when the surprising letters came.

The suspense builds from this first sentence to a very satisfactory conclusion. Curiosity and the need to help a relative in distress are sufficient reasons for Sally, Amy, and Jack to persuade their mother to drive them to the Georgia coast for a visit with Uncle Will and a search for treasure. At Uncle Will's run-down house, the sleuthing begins. Each clue brings a new treasure, but as the hunt progresses, it is discovered that the most significant clue is the hardest of all to unravel.

162 St. John, Wylly Folk. *Uncle Robert's Secret.* Illus.   **(I)**
by Frank Aloise. Viking, 1972. 159p.

> We might have heard more of his plans that night, (but) then the old tub we were standing on gave way.

The story centers around Debbie; her younger brother, Sonny; and older brother, Bob, who is referred to as "Uncle Bob" due to his anticipation of being uncle to older sister Betsy's child. When Betsy moves away, Bob shelters another child that has been abused by his parents. There is a puzzling link between the criminal couple and elderly Mr. Peregrine who lives next door to the youngsters. After high adventure and narrow escapes, the link is explained. This is a no-let-up suspense and pure-fun story set in Georgia.

163   Scholefield, Edmund O. *Yankee Boy.* Illus. by   (J)
          Lewis W. Gordon. World, 1971. 152p.

> ". . . I want a word with you, boy," the old man said, and Ted for a moment thought he'd done something wrong.

Ted, who had always lived in New York City, is sent to live with his new stepmother's family in rural Alabama. The development of mutual affection between the Alabama farmer and the New York teenager provides good reading for young adults of today. *Yankee Boy* merges two worlds to make a heartwarming story about a boy and his growing respect for a way of life he had never known.

164   Searcy, Margaret Zehmer. *Ikwa of the Temple*   (J)
          Mounts. Illus. Univ. of Alabama Pr., 1974. unp.

> Ikwa, you are getting old enough to learn the ways of a woman.

Ikwa's life is action-filled as she grows into womanhood and learns the rituals required in becoming a woman of the mound builders. Ways of the tribe in which her brother and cousins are trained are also described. Drawings help bring the life within an Indian village into reality for the reader, as do the photographs from Moundville State Park.

165   Seton, Anya. *Devil Water.* Houghton, 1962. 526p.   (S)
          (Paperback ed., Fawcett World, 1976)

> And what had he ever really done for Jenny except entangle her in doom?

Charles Radcliffe escaped from Newgate prison only to be executed later before a London mob. Set in England and Virginia in the early eighteenth century, this novel based on facts about Charles Radcliffe; Jenny, his daughter by a secret marriage; two Jacobite rebellions; and the family of William Byrd of Westover centers around the strong affection between father and daughter which endured not only years of separation but conflicting beliefs and loyalties. Life, manners, and customs in eighteenth-century England and Virginia are described in detail.

166   Seton, Anya.   *My Theodosia.*   Houghton, 1941.   **(S)**
423p.   (Paperback ed., Pyramid, 1975)

The Patriot rolled sluggishly for the last time as though weary of her fruitless struggle.

In 1812, Theodosia, daughter of Aaron Burr, sailed from Georgetown aboard the packet *The Patriot* bound for New York to visit her father, whom she had not seen since his exile. Her disappearance at sea is still an unsolved mystery. Readers of this fictionalized biography will be fascinated by the tragic heroine Theodosia as she plays her part against a stage peopled with such historical characters as Meriwether Lewis, the Madisons, Thomas Jefferson, and Washington Irving. The book includes a number of letters which should be useful to high school history students.

167   Sharpe, Stella Gentry.   *Tobe.*   Photographs by   **(P, I)**
Charles Farrell.   Univ. of North Carolina Pr., 1939.
121p.

Sometimes Mother and Daddy tell us stories and sing until we can't keep our eyes open.

Black-and-white photographs give depth and realism to this easy-to-read story of a six-year-old black boy and his family living on a farm in North Carolina. Tobe and his five brothers' experiences as they work, play, enjoy holidays, and roam in the woods are all described in this account of an enterprising black farm family.

168   Shelton, William R.   *Stowaway to the Moon: the*   **(S)**
Camelot Odyssey.   Doubleday, 1973.   343p.

The transmission ended. The one-man jury had voted. And the vote was against them all.

E. J. Mackernutt, Jr., eleven years old, of Titusville, Florida, realized his dream of space flight by stowing away aboard the spacecraft *Camelot,* endangering its lunar mission and the entire space program. Ultimately, however, his presence leads to a reappraisal of man's place in the universe. Warm and believable human relationships, a logical story line, close attention to technical details, and an unusually true-to-life feeling for Florida's natural history help make E. J.'s incredible adventure an exciting tale.

169   Sibley, Celestine.   *Christmas in Georgia.*   Illus. by   **(I, J, S)**
Scarlett Rickenbaker.   Doubleday, 1964.   95p.

The rain that Old Stovelid Mountain had moaned about the night before had begun to fall. . . .

The quotation above illustrates the charm of the writing of these tales, which range in time from the revolutionary war to the present and in locale from a seacoast island to the Blue Ridge Mountains. As was the case in her previous book, *Peachtree Street, U.S.A.*, the appeal of the five tales is so strong and of such a timely, universal nature that they are enjoyed by all ages everywhere.

170   Singmaster, Elsie. *You Make Your Own Luck*. Illus.   (J, S)
      by Bernard Westmacott. Longmans, 1929. 225p.   op

> There was a spool bed, a splint chair . . . and a small table on which stood a basin.

On a summer day in the early 1920s, sixteen-year-old Nellie Edna felt trapped in her native valley of Virginia. The chance remark of a tourist opened her eyes to all the possibilities in her future if she would only make an effort. Leaving the shelter of Aunt Myra's tourist home, she went to teach in a mountain school and awakened to an appreciation of her surroundings. The description of the people and customs in the 1920s, as well as during the earlier history of the region is interesting and accurate.

171   Slaughter, Frank G. *Apalachee Gold*. Doubleday,   (J, S)
      1954. 254p.

> Swaying on his perch at the prow, Pedro watched the canoes glide over the water toward them.

Based on extensive research, this fictionalized account of "the fabulous adventures of Cabeza de Vaca" takes Pedro Morales, de Vaca's nephew and clerk, from the expedition's beginning in Havana through the landing in south Florida, and on the long trek across the Florida wilderness where the explorers were alternately welcomed and attacked by various Indian tribes. Finally they reached New Spain (now Mexico) without ever finding the long-sought gold of Apalachee. A slight romantic theme may make the novel more appealing to some readers. The Author's Notes give recommended sources for further study.

172   Smith, Doris Buchanan. *Kelly's Creek*. Illus. by Alan   (I)
      Tiegreen. Crowell, 1975. 70p.

> The straw-gold of the late-winter marsh matched his hair and eyes and freckles.

Kelly is a typical nine-year-old boy except for his slowness in learning. His main interests in life are the marshes and the seashore. He meets and becomes friends with a marine biology student from nearby Brunswick Junior College. The story concerns Kelly's difficulties and the way in which his interest in marine life plus Phillip's assistance help him overcome these problems.

173   Smith, Doris Buchanan.   *Kick a Stone Home.*   (I, J)
      Crowell, 1974. 152p.

> Outside, a sun that promised spring to the world failed to lighten her mood.

Fifteen-year-old Sara learns to overcome her shyness, especially with boys, and to accept herself. But this is not the usual tomboy turns feminine story since it has real characters who develop believably and descriptions which portray accurately the story's south Georgia setting. It is satisfyingly romantic, yet closely concerned with the formation of Sara's new self-image, which she tests against interested boys, her friends, teachers, and divorced parents.

174   Smith, Doris Buchanan.   *A Taste of Blackberries.*   (I)
      Illus. by Charles Robinson.   Crowell, 1973. 58p.

> Sometimes Jamie made me sick. I twisted the lid onto my beetle jar and put it down.

Jamie is stung by a bee and falls screaming and writhing to the ground. His best friend disgustedly stalks off, only to learn later that Jamie is dead. The boy feels guilty because he thought Jamie was clowning and did not try to help him. After the funeral he comes to grips with the tragedy and learns to manage his grief. The difficult and sensitive subject is treated with taste and honesty. The story could have happened anywhere, but the author draws heavily on the south Georgia background she knows best.

175   Smith, Doris Buchanan.   *Tough Chauncey.*   (I, J)
      Frontispiece by Michael Eagle.   Morrow, 1974.
      222p.

> In fact, even when he was innocent, someone could point at him for blame and he was in trouble.

Abused by his grandfather and neglected by his mother, tough thirteen-year-old Chauncey decides running away from his south Georgia home is the only solution to changing his life until a friend shows him another alternative. A remarkably intimate story of identity search, valuable both for tough Chaunceys and those who would better understand them.

176   Smith, Edith Hutchins.   *Drought and Other North*   (S)
          Carolina Yarns.   Illus. by Elizabeth Toth Spencer.
          Blair, 1955.   153p.

> Tractors just ain't got the natural climbing ability of a good Carolina
> mule.

In the eleven stories in this collection, the author very successfully
conveys a humorous glimpse of small town life in the early years of this
decade. "Invasion" is a down-south version of *Aladdin's Lamp*, with
Grandma renaming the genie, Joe. "City Gal" gives the reader a small
town, early 1940 version of women's lib. "Cordwood" tells about a
typical North Carolina boy and some of his experiences after he left
Fort Bragg and met the enemy. Teenagers should enjoy these southern
yarns.

177   Snow, Dorothea J.   *The Secret of the Stone Frog.*   (I)
          Illus. by Raymond Burns.   Bobbs-Merrill, 1959.
          215p.

> Boy, I wish that old frog could talk!

Billy Joe is distressed when he learns that his family is returning
to Alabama. His disappointment is brief when he finds a forgotten and
hidden cave whose secret has been kept by a rock formation which re-
sembles a frog. This is an action-filled story of a ten-year-old boy who
finds the solution to a double mystery and in the process learns a great
deal about people and human nature.

178   Sorensen, Virginia.   *Curious Missie.*   Illus. by Marilyn   (I)
          Miller.   Harcourt, 1953.   208p.

> Missie heard somebody say, "That's Curious Missie. They call her
> the Little Girl who got the County Bookmobile."

A little rural Alabama girl loves asking questions and her ambition is to grow big enough to use the schoolroom shelf marked "library."
The way in which her community uses her to sell the county government on the idea of a county bookmobile is an engrossing story.

179   Stahl, Ben.   *Blackbeard's Ghost.*   Houghton, 1965.   (I, J)
          184p.

> "Yup," said Teach, "Parched maise be the stuff to raise a swab's
> thirst, I always say."

J. D. and Hank, fourteen-year-old students at Goldolphin Junior
High school, team up with the ghost of Edward Teach (the infamous
Pirate Blackbeard) to confuse and bewitch the work crews attempting

to tear down the famous Old Boar's Head Tavern. The forces of preservation overcome those of progress and the Tavern is saved. Background history of the North Carolina seaport, where the tale is set; its invasion by the pirate crew; and the intrigue between Blackbeard and Governor Eden which led to the building of Old Boar's Head Tavern are given in the Prologue. The Epilogue serves to give a final summation of the episode. Artistically illustrated with the author's black-and-white drawings, this readable, exciting story should appeal especially to teenage boys.

180   Steele, William O. *Tomahawk Border*. Illus. by   (I, J)
      Vernon Wooten. Colonial Williamsburg, 1966. 120p.

    I had my doubts about you, at times, Rogers, but you've made a good ranger.

At sixteen, Delk Rogers ran away from the farm to join the rangers; but his careless, irresponsible attitude caused them to turn against him. Delk's fight to regain their trust and respect is an exciting story of his growth into manhood as a Virginia ranger on the southwestern frontier in the early eighteenth century.

181   Steele, William O. *Wayah of the Real People*. Illus.   (I, J)
      by Isa Barnett. Colonial Williamsburg, 1964. 128p.

    He, Wayah, the Wolf, was going among the white men. . . .

The Cherokees (the Real People) of Chota were sending Wayah for one year to attend the Bafferton School for Indians at Williamsburg. Because Otonee had said the white men were evil and because the Cherokees hated them, Wayah did not want to go. But trade with the Virginians was promised to the Chota village if they would send a boy to Williamsburg. Without the Virginians' trade Chota was doomed. How Wayah survives the year in the white man's world and how it changes him is the subject of this exciting and understanding novel.

182   Stewart, John Craig. *Muscogee Twilight*. American   (J, S)
      Southern, 1964. 132p.

    Far down in the southern section of what is now Alabama. . . .

Most of what is known about the Creek Indians is legend. However, the military genius of the Red Eagle, William Weatherford, and his love for a white girl are facts not only known to be true, but which make this a very interesting story.

183   Stolz, Mary. *Lands End*. Illus. by Dennis   (I, J)
      Hermanson. Harper, 1973. 208p.

He watched a pelican skim low over the water, wingtips barely clearing the waves.

Twelve-year-old Josh is much at ease with nature on the Florida Gulf Coast island where he lives, but sometimes he has problems relating to other people, especially his parents. When the easygoing Arthur family comes to the island, Josh learns to better understand both himself and his world. Well-drawn characters, believable human relationships, gentle humor, sensitive descriptions of Florida's natural beauty, and an understated but definite environmental message help make this story of a youth's growing pains one to which young people will relate.

184 Street, James, and Tracy, Don. *Pride of Possession.* (S)
Lippincott, 1960. 281p.

His two oaths: one almost sworn to his father and the other, the new one, that he was bound to fulfill, the promise to get Fiefield Bald back.

Although a year had passed since the hunting accident in which his father had died, Kiah McCable still carried the haunting memory of his father's eyes filled with disappointment. Ridden with guilt at his own failure to stop the boar which gored Braith McCable to death, Kiah had resisted changes. He finally comes to terms with the past in a dramatic confrontation.

185 Styron, William. *The Confessions of Nat Turner, A* (S)
Novel. Random, 1967. 429p. (Paperback ed., New American Library, 1968)

Confess that thy acts may be known to all men.

In August, 1831, in a remote part of southeastern Virginia, the only effective sustained slave revolt in American history took place. The story of the rebellion and Nat's life history are narrated by Nat, himself, in his jail cell as he awaits his trial and execution. His religious zeal, his hatred of the whites, and the events of his life which led him to plan the insurrection are all revealed in an agonizing retelling of the pain and horror of slavery. Winner of a Pulitzer Prize, this is a book for mature readers.

186 Sutton, Felix. *We Were There at the First Airplane* (J)
Flight. (We Were There Series) Grosset & Dunlap, 1960. 179p.

Jimmy watches closely as Wilbur's skillful fingers re-sewed the silk over the ribs.

A young North Carolinian meets the Wright brothers and becomes involved in their attempts to launch a motorized aircraft at

Kitty Hawk, North Carolina. This fictionalized version of events leading up to the famous flight will appeal to teenage flying buffs.

187 Tate, Allen. *Jefferson Davis, His Rise and Fall: A*   (J, S)
         Biographical Narrative. Illus. Putnam, 1969. 189p.

> . . . So Jefferson Davis and the Southern Confederacy fell.

The author delves into the many faceted causes of the Civil War,
citing forces moving in Europe as well as in the United States. He
shows Davis as a bit of a "hot-head," but grants the president of the
Confederacy some degree of honor. A useful index is included.

188 Thane, Elswyth. *Dawn's Early Light.* Duell, 1943.   (J, S)
         317p. (Paperback ed., Dell, 1972)

> I am not your sister! . . . I'm not even kissing kin to you.

This pleasant romantic story set in Williamsburg, Virginia, adequately describes the challenges of the opening of a new country, both
geographically and politically. The fictional figures are interwoven with
those historical personalities who molded the character of the country
during the time of the Revolution.

189 Thane, Elswyth. *Yankee Stranger.* Hawthorn, 1975.   (J, S)
         306p.

> Nothing Eden had experienced in Williamsburg . . . prepared her for
> that July day in Richmond.

Williamsburg in the autumn of 1860 was tense. When a Yankee
arrived there and Eden Day fell in love with him, their relationship was
not well accepted in view of the ongoing political struggle between
North and South. The action moves from Williamsburg to Richmond
to Washington and covers the span of the Civil War. Historical figures
such as Lee, Jackson, and Stuart are seen through the eyes of the men
whom they led. This action-packed romance presents an accurate picture of life during the Civil War.

190 Thompson, Wesley S. *So Turns the Tide.* Pareil   (S)
         Press, 1965. 264p.   op

> Within the heart of Wayne Haskell there burned the light of in-
> spiration.

Readers will be touched by this poignant story of the conflict
within the hearts and minds of the people in North Alabama during the
Civil War. Their struggles and hardships are realistically told, and the
grace and dignity of Southern society give a romantic element to the
story.

191 Tyler, Anne. *If Morning Ever Comes.* Knopf, 1965. (S)
266p.

Seems like you are always loving the people that fly away from you,
Ben Joe, and flying away from the people that you love.

Ben Joe Hawkes returns to his home in Sandhill, North Carolina,
from New York, where he is a law student at Columbia University,
when the oldest of his six sisters leaves her husband and comes home.
As the only man in a family of women, he feels responsible for their
well-being. To his surprise, he finds they are managing very well on
their own, and he must readjust his attitude toward the family. The
conflict and character development make interesting reading while presenting a vivid picture of North Carolina small town life today.

192 Vinson, Kathryn. *Run With the Ring.* Harcourt, (S)
1965. 225p.

With cumulative intensity the word swelled to a crescendo that
could not be denied. Blindness!

When high school track star Mark Mansfield is blinded in a running accident, he is filled with bitterness and despair. Seeking independence from his family, he enters a school for the blind. The change
in his life is traumatic, but he learns to accept his limitations and find
new strengths and abilities. Despite a rather farfetched climax, the
story of his struggle is told authentically and sympathetically. Although fictionalized, the setting is recognizable as Saint Augustine and
the Florida School for the Deaf and Blind.

193 Waldron, Ann. *The Luckie Star.* Dutton, 1977. (I, J)
166p.

There were pictures of gold coins like hers in the book.

Another summer at the family's north Florida beach cottage was
not what Quincy wanted this year. She much preferred to stay in
Houston and attend summer science classes at Rice University, but being the youngest in the family she was not allowed that privilege. To
her surprise, however, the summer's adventures served to enhance her
scientific knowledge and helped her family appreciate the interest she
had in astronomical phenomena. Accurate ecological information and
excellent descriptive treatment of the north Florida Gulf Coast make
this a useful work as well as a good story.

194 Wellman, Manly Wade. *Battle for King's Mountain.* (S)
Washburn, 1962. 170p.

Deep summertime along the South Fork in the Carolina Piedmont
was beautiful.

Continuing the exciting tale begun in his earlier work, *Rifles at Ransour's Mill*, Wellman shows how Continental Army scout, Zack Harper, followed the Tories under Colonel Patrick Ferguson across North Carolina to the famous battle at King's Mountain. This realistic account of the scouting, fighting, and personal encounters between Loyalists and revolutionary sympathizers should appeal especially to high school students. The story is based on actual records of the War of Independence and sources are given.

195 Wellman, Manly Wade. *Carolina Pirate.*   (S)
      Washburn, 1968. 167p.

Plainly the Captain was far the better swordsman of the two, thought Ranald, and could dispose of Shoup at any moment he wished.

Ranald Blaikie had never seen a pirate until his father's ship was commandeered in 1741 by a band of pirates fleeing the Spanish. In return for his services as navigator, a duty usually performed by the injured pirate leader, Ranald's crew and passengers were released and the young sailor began an adventure as a somewhat unwilling pirate in the Atlantic. Although there is plenty of swashbuckling action, Captain Haws and his band are far from bloodthirsty, often releasing captives and even aiding British marines against a Spanish warship.

196 Wellman, Manley Wade. *Settlement on Shocco.*   (J, S)
      Blair, 1963. 184p.

It will take us southward, toward that creek called Shocco, where our land lies.

Frontier living is vividly described in this exciting story of the Edward Jones family as they move from their successful plantation in Tidewater Virginia to the wilderness of Warren County, North Carolina. Especially interesting is the account of the surveying of the property by young Sugan and James Jones and the way in which the conniving tavern-keeper Destin used forged papers to try to steal the Jones's property. A brief resume of events on Shocco Creek up to the present time is given in the Historical Note at the close of the story.

197 Wellman, Manly Wade. *Young Squire Morgan.*   (I)
      Washburn, 1956. 172p.

The big yellow-bearded backwoodsman in fringed shirt and broad hat was making too much noise. . . .

Frontier days in Alabama are well portrayed in this tale of adventure and intrigue. Jason wants to be a lawyer (called squire in the 1830s). His quick thinking saves the life of Squire Colquit with whom he later studies law. He becomes deeply involved in a case in which the results are as surprising to the reader as they are to Jason.

198 West, John Foster. *Appalachian Dawn.* Moore,   (S)
1973. 191p.

> The horse, now rested, cantered down the crest of the ridge and entered the woods.

Beginning with a realistic account of John Ward's birth in a backwoods cabin, this sequel to *Time Was* concerns itself with the first ten years of the life of this sensitive, mountaineer boy. Guided by the love and folk-wisdom of his mother as well as the warm acceptance of his older brothers and sisters, John is able to cope with his aging father's rejection and learns to understand himself as he finds his place in the world. The final chapter brings John Ward back to his childhood homes where he philosophizes as to their effects on his life. The mountain dialect may be difficult for readers not accustomed to this pattern of speech.

199 Whitney, Phyllis A. *Lost Island.* Doubleday, 1970.   (J, S)
252p.

> There's nothing so achingly painful as childhood longing for something not altogether understood.

Lacy Ames returns to the old plantation on Hampton Island off the coast of Georgia and remembers the fun, pain, and loves of childhood. She also feels "a pervading sense of evil." She discovers that nine-year-old Richard, son of Gill Severn whom she secretly loves, is really not her cousin Elise's son at all, but Aunt Amalie refuses to divulge the secret of his real mother. During the annual Camelot Ball, sudden death and the emotions and events triggered thereby begin to resolve the conflicts and mysteries.

200 Wibberley, Leonard. *John Treegate's Musket.*   (J, S)
Farrar, 1959. 188p.

> He left me here as a child to go to England. . . .

This was the feeling of eleven-year-old Peter Treegate as his father went to England on business. Peter becomes involved in a murder on the docks of Boston and fleeing from the police ends up on a cargo ship. The ship, *Maid of Malden,* is wrecked by a hurricane off the coast of South Carolina. Peter rejoins his father six years later with the help of a Scotsman named Maclaren of Spey, who found Peter after the shipwreck. Together father and son prepare to fight at the Battle of Bunker Hill. A vivid picture of the military and political activities in Boston and South Carolina during the colonial period is presented through this exciting story.

201 Wier, Ester. *The Winners.* Illus. by Ursula Koering.   (I, J, S)
McKay, 1967. 179p.

> "You're one of them worthless ones that nothin' ever goes right for. You're a born loser. . . ."

Young Scrub Nolan was sent by his father, a migrant worker, to stay with an aunt in Florida, but he ends up lost in the Everglades. Robbed of both his money and his self-respect, Scrub finds new friends in Johnny, the Indian boy, and Cap, the hermit. Together, they live in harmony with the wilderness, trying to thwart the poachers who prey on the endangered wildlife. When they enter Cap's swamp buggy in the annual race at Naples, Scrub finally finds out what makes a winner.

202 Wilkinson, Brenda. *Ludell.* Harper, 1975. 170p.   (I, J)

> It's your own lil' red wagon. You can roll it, pull it, or drag it. . . .

This was the teacher's advice to Ludell Wilson, whom the reader first meets as she is daydreaming in class: there wasn't "anythang" to get excited about until Friday. The biggest dream in Ludell's "worle" was for her mother to keep her promise to send a "tee-vee"—a big dream for a poor, black kid during the fifties in Waycross, Georgia. The concerns, embarrassments, sufferings, pranks, and hobbies of Ludell lead her to take up reading, which in turn brings her to high school and her development into a promising writer.

203 Wilkinson, Sylvia. *Moss on the North Side.*   (S)
Houghton, 1966. 235p.

> The woods are dark since the light of the sunset can't come through the trees.

Cary, the illegitimate daughter of a North Carolina tenant farmer, struggles to find her place in the community after the death of her Indian father. Rejecting any help from her socially outcast mother, she finds strength in the things of nature which her father had taught her to love and respect. This is a highly emotional, sometimes psychological novel which will appeal mainly to the more mature student—especially those interested in North Carolina wildlife.

204 Williams, Ben Ames. *House Divided.* Houghton,   (S)
1947. 1,514p.

> The Currains, through their Courdian forebears, had been Virginians for a hundred and fifty years. . . .

With plantations in Virginia, North and South Carolina, and houses in Richmond, the Currain family and their political and social life give an interesting perspective of the history of the United States. General James Longstreet's role in the Civil War is detailed as it is woven into the story through his friendship with members of the family. Although the length of this narrative might deter some from reading it, the story holds the reader's interest to the end. Richmond in a flurry of wartime activities and as a ravaged city is graphically pictured.

205 Williams, Maxville Burt. *First for Freedom.* Moore,   (J, S)
1976. 312p.

"If we are to be the first for Freedom—SO BE IT," said Harnett.

North Carolinians have long been proud that their "declaration of independence" preceded the one adopted by all the colonies. This fictional account chronicles the events from the writing of the Halifax Resolves in April, 1776, to the defeat of Cornwallis at Yorktown, South Carolina, as witnessed by a young man of Halifax. While the style of writing tends to understate the excitement and suspense that could be conveyed, the historical sequence is carefully followed. Illustrations emphasize important leaders and historical sites. Village and plantation life are pictured as well. Despite the fact that this account may be a bit long for younger readers it is easy to comprehend. An outdoor drama based on the work was presented in Halifax in June, 1976, by the Halifax Historical Association.

206 Wolfe, Thomas. *Look Homeward, Angel.* Scribner,   (S)
1929. 626p.

Below him a mountain stream foamed down its rocky bed . . . across the hill toward Altamont.

This first novel by one of North Carolina's most famous writers is a lengthy, earthy saga of a young man's search for his place in his family, his town or village, his country, and finally his world. Descriptions of everyday life in Altamont (Asheville, North Carolina) and the surrounding mountain areas give realistic pictures of life in the early 1900s when trains, streetcars, and summer boarding houses were all part of the life-style in this section of the country. Because of its length and philosophical approach to life, this book will appeal to the more mature, gifted reader.

207 Wooley, Catherine. *Ginnie and the Mystery Light.*   (I)
Morrow, 1973. 191p.

Some distance from them, down the road, a bright light was shining.

Ginnie's curiosity about this strange and mysterious light on Lonesome Bay Road leads her to adventure and suspense during her holiday visit to Charleston, South Carolina. The reader is in for a surprise-filled tale as Ginnie and her friends try to discover what is causing an unusual, reappearing light that has baffled and frightened the superstitious inhabitants of the area. This fictitious story is based on a true experience.

FOLKTALES

208 Arnold, Lattye Eunice. *Aunt Malissa's Memory Jug.* (I, J)
Exposition, 1962. 141p.

> You put this one good eyeglass on the Memory Jug, so you will not forget Mis' Adelaide.

A memory jug, according to the author, is a large jug which is covered with plaster-of-paris, into which small keepsakes are pressed while the plaster is wet. These mementos serve as reminders of events and people of the past. The stories in this collection are based on the souvenirs collected on one such jug. They give a picture of rural life and customs of the last generation. Local dialect is used where appropriate.

209 Bolick, Julian Stevenson. *Ghosts from the Coast: A* (J, S)
Collection of Twelve Stories from Georgetown County,
South Carolina. Jacobs, 1966. 158p.

> Blood, glowing like phosphorous in the uncanny crosslights, was oozing from the open wound.

This collection of twelve legends and ghost stories range from the tragic to the humorous. In this, his third collection of Georgetown folklore, Bolick reminds us that ghosts have one common affinity: noisily they insist on being noticed. The ghost stories were gathered from storytellers now ghosts themselves; legends were handed over from one family to another. The author's pen and ink drawings enrich the format and authentically capture the mood and character of each story. Other illustrations, resembling woodcuts, convey plainly that the old coastal houses were meant to be haunted—framed as they are by live oak thickets from whose branches hang streamers of Spanish moss.

210 Bolick, Julian Stevenson. *The Return of the Gray* (I, J, S)
Man, and Georgetown Ghosts. Jacobs, 1956. 175p.

> It appeared to her that she caught a glimpse of a white-clad figure fading through the door. . . .

This collection of Carolina folklore is centered around the Gray Man of Pawley's Island and other ghosts of Waccamaw Neck and Georgetown County. These coastal ghost tales are full of history and tradition intertwined with romance and mystery. They were obtained from descendants of plantation slaves, planters, overseers, and fishermen. Each is based upon historic fact though many had to be pieced together from bits gathered from several sources. Most of the characters of the stories are sad, good persons who met with untimely deaths. Most made their posthumous appearances as forerunners of good tidings or bearers of storm warnings and, as such, were welcomed rather than feared by those who encountered them. A short prologue prefacing each story informs the reader about location, characters, and pertinent history. The author's pen and ink sketches add much to the overall flavor of quaintness and romance created throughout the book.

211 Botkin, B. A., ed. *A Treasury of Southern Folklore:* (S)
Stories, Ballads, Traditions and Folkways of the People
of the South. Crown, 1949. 776p.

The Washington of folklore will . . . be the boy who was credited with throwing a dollar across the Rappahannock.

Folktales and folksongs about Virginia's heroes, traditions, history, and people from the Tidewater to the Blue Ridge are included. A collection of probably the best known folklore Virginia and the other Southern states have to offer. An index of authors, titles, and first lines of songs as well as an index of subjects, names, and places are included.

212 Brookes, Stella Brower. *Joel Chandler Harris:* (S)
Folklorist. Univ. of Georgia Pr., 1950. 182p.

Dar's a heap er ups an' downs in his worl', mo' speshually downs.

The above quotation is one of the proverbs contained in this volume which covers an account of Harris as a folklorist, and an analysis of his tales, proverbs, and songs. Part I deals with material concerning the influences during his early years prior to the publication of the first Uncle Remus book in 1880. Part II is an analysis of his folklore arranged under the headings of Trickster Tales, Myths, Supernatural Tales, Proverbs, Dialect, and Songs. The appendix contains an index to the location of the Uncle Remus tales, an article about the folklore of southern blacks, a bibliography of books and magazine articles by and about Harris, and notes concerning this book.

213 Chaney, James A., ed. *Carolina Country Reader.* (S)
Moore, 1973. 269p.

Time stood still, letting the old linger and the young vaguely imagine how their years would be.

These articles from the magazine *Carolina Country* do more than make time stand still. Subjects range from folk songs to state history; from Mother's Day to Christmas; from the customs of the mountain folk to the folkways of the coastal region. It is a rich collection which includes poetry, humor, nostalgia, and folklore—a collection which reflects the varied population of North Carolina.

214 Chase, Richard, ed. *Grandfather Tales.* Illus. by   (I, J)
Berkeley Williams, Jr. Houghton, 1948. 240p.

And they thought he'd done got witched and was runnin' crazy.

In this collection, Mr. Chase has "put each tale together from different versions" which he heard in the mountains of the southeastern United States. Familiar tales are told with a definite flavor of the region in which they were found. Musical scores are included when needed and Williams's line drawings add interest and depth to the prose. Sources for the various versions of the tales are given in the appendix.

215 Chase, Richard. *Jack and the Three Sillies.* Illus.   (P)
by Joshua Tolford. Houghton, 1950. 40p.

Jack was lazy. He didn't want to walk all the way to the settlement with that cow.

Attractive colored drawings give a realistic picture of Jack's mountain farm home and add humor to this simple retelling of one of the favorite folktales of the Blue Ridge Mountains.

216 Chase, Richard, ed. *The Jack Tales.* Illus. by   (I, J)
Berkeley Williams, Jr. Houghton, 1943. 202p.

This here's another tale about Jack when he was still a small-like boy.

This collection of tales about the well-known folk hero, Jack, was "told by R. M. Ward and his kindred in the Beech Mt. section of Western North Carolina; and other descendants of Council Harmon (1803-1896)." In a very interesting preface, Mr. Chase gives the reader a background for the tales and a bit of his philosophy on the importance of preserving our oral heritage. Eighteen stories are recounted in the collection, including such old favorites as "Jack and the Giants," "Newground," "Jack and the Bean Tree," "Big Jack and Little Jack," and "Jack and the Doctor's Girl." Attractive line drawings enhance the regional flavor of the stories' settings. An appendix, compiled by Herbert Halpert, gives an in-depth discourse on folktales and their importance in our literature. The list of "Parallel Tales" with their sources will appeal to serious folklore students. An alphabetical glossary defines those regional colloquialisms which might be unfamiliar to the average reader.

217   Credle, Ellis.   *Big Fraid, Little Fraid.*   Nelson, 1964.   (P)
unp.

There on the fence sat a frightful little something, he didn't know what. . . .

This humorous folktale, delightfully illustrated with the author's yellow and brown drawings, was a favorite told him by a great-uncle, Alfred Cooper, while they waited for the mail in Nash County, North Carolina. In the tale Little Chub is the Cullifer family jokester, and he keeps things lively with his practical jokes. When his brother Dave decides to "give him his come-uppance" by pretending to be one of the "fraids," a monkey joins in the fun. The postscript gives an interesting essay on early American humor.

218   Credle, Ellis.   *Tall Tales from the High Hills.*   (J, S)
Nelson, 1957.   156p.

Before she knew what was happening, she was tumbling head over heels inside that pumpkin as it rolled out of the cornfield.

Exaggeration is a primary ingredient of mountain humor, demonstrating the mountaineer's imaginative outlook and providing many an hour of entertainment in "swapping tales." Some of the tales included here have been passed along from days past, but some might have happened yesterday in a little town just down the road. In each one, a problem is solved in a highly original, creative way. Does it matter if it didn't really happen that way at all?

219   Davis, Burke.   *Roberta E. Lee.*   Illus. by John Opper.   (I)
John J. Blair, 1956.   unp.

This book is for children, or people who have been children. Others keep out. Barefoot County law forbids trespassing.

A humorous, tongue-in-cheek, picture book about a southern-belle rabbit who "longed to be prettier than Scarlett O'Hara or anybody else." U. S. Terrapin did all he could to improve Roberta's looks. With the help of the Beauty Stretcher he gave her the long legs and ears for which rabbits are famous, even though in the process her long tail was turned into a mere cotton puff.

220   *Foxfire 2.*   Ed. with an introduction by Eliot   (J, S)
Wigginton.   Doubleday, 1973.   406p.

"Honey is described as 'larrupin' good; and a man ain't tasted nothin' 'lessen he's put his tongue to sourwood honey."

The above quotation illustrates how high school pupils tell the story of the north Georgia mountains in the language of the people they interview. The stories in *Foxfire 2* as well as *Foxfire Book* and *Foxfire 3* first appeared in the class-written and published magazine *Foxfire*. All areas of farm life are covered, with photographs, including "ghost stories, spring wild plant foods, spinning and weaving, midwifing, burial customs, cornshuckin's, wagon making, and many more affairs of plain living."

221   Green, Paul.   *Home to My Valley.*   Univ. of North   (I, J, S)
Carolina Pr., 1970.   140p.

You know that's an interesting thing about people, they all enjoy stories. Whether they're sad or funny, they enjoy 'em just so there's a tale in 'em.

Paul Green is a master storyteller, a fact evidenced in this collection of stories from the Cape Fear River Valley of North Carolina. Folklore, local character sketches, and autobiographical accounts are told with an understanding and appreciation for the people of the region and their ways, which Green has learned to value during his days of traveling in the Cape Fear area.

222   Harden, John.   *The Devil's Tramping Ground and*   (I, J, S)
Other North Carolina Mystery Stories.   Univ. of North
Carolina Pr., 1940.   178p.

The Devil goes there to walk in circles as he thinks up new means of causing trouble for humanity.

These North Carolina mysteries were originally broadcast as a radio series called "Tales of Tar Heelia." The stories, written in an easy-to-read style, come from all parts of the state and range in time from Raleigh's Lost Colony to the modern-day disappearance of an army major. Some are true folktales, full of superstition and legend, while others concern people (and animals) whose lives can be documented. The author gives all the evidence available about these mystery tales, leaving the reader to form his own opinions.

223   Jagendorf, Moritz Adolph.   *Folk Stories of the South.*   (I, J)
Vanguard, 1972.   355p.

I have come here to offer my services, sir, to carry any message you wish.

These were words spoken by Emily Geiger in the tale "Emily's Famous Meal," a story of courage and daring. When the revolutionary war began, Emily volunteered her services and was entrusted with a message to General Sumter. This account of Emily's escape from spies during her journey to the general is only one of the eight tales about South Carolina in this book. Most of the South Carolina stories are set in Charleston, Beaufort, and surrounding areas. Also included are myths, ghost stories, tales of magic, strong-man tales, and adventures of war heroines. The collection is arranged alphabetically by states.

224 Killion, Ronald G., and Walker, Charles T. *A*   (J, S)
Treasury of Georgia Folklore. Illus. by Maureen
O'Leary. Cherokee, 1972. 267p.

To make a woman drop dead, take nine hairs. . . .

So begins one of the conjure tales. In addition to these tales, the book contains the games children played, tales of haunted houses, Indian legends, rules for planting and harvesting, superstitions, and folk medicine. This is a delightful book which will both entertain and inform the reader. It is well indexed.

225 Malcolmson, Anne. *Yankee Doodle's Cousins.* Illus.   (I, J)
by Robert McCloskey. Houghton, 1941. 267p.

I'm not a bad fellow, after all, boys. What's a little prank between friends?

Blackbeard, the pirate, was described as a noted prankster in this collection of folk hero stories. The stories are arranged by sections of the country, from east to west. The five stories from the south include the famous Blackbeard and John Henry tales. McCloskey's delightful illustrations add to the appeal of the stories. Folk hero stories can help children identify with the democratic, industrial civilization that is America.

226 Morgan, Fred T. *Uwharrie Magic.* Moore, 1974.   (J, S)
215p.

Ghosts used to sit on the front porch and talk with old Uncle Abraham Shadd at his two-story home on the banks of Haw Branch near the foot of Lick Mountain.

Some of the folktales in this collection are based on legends, some on the experiences of real people, and the author brings them all to life in the retelling. Witches, ghosts, monsters, superstitions, and strange occurrences are part of the rich oral tradition of the Uwharrie region of North Carolina. These stories give insights into the background and life-styles of the inhabitants and will provide the reader some thrills as well.

227   Newell, David M.   *If Nothin' Don't Happen.*   Illus.   (S)
      by Mark Livingston.   Knopf, 1975.   242p.

> When I were seven years old I seen Daddy kill a yearlin' bear eighty
> steps away. . . .

Billy Driggers narrates this collection of stories and tall tales
which form a loosely woven account of growing up in the backwoods
of the Gulf Hammock-Withlacoochee River country of Florida during
the early years of the twentieth century. The Driggers family and their
neighbors live close to nature, and their lives center around farming,
hunting, and fishing. Written from the author's personal experience
with the region and with the outdoors, these colorful and authentic
cracker stories are sometimes dramatic, often lusty, usually hilarious,
and generally entertaining.

228   Parris, John.   *Mountain Bred.*   Illus. by Dorothy   (J, S)
      Luxton Parris.   *Asheville Citizen-Times,* 1967.   372p.

> The smell of the wood smoke blended with the spicy smell of apples
> cooking.

This collection of more than 125 of the author's newspaper columns on folkways and mountain tales was printed "to satisfy the hun-
dreds of requests received" for copies of his now out-of-print *Roaming
of the Mountains* and *My Mountains, My People.* John Parris's descriptive, sympathetic style of writing brings the reader in close contact
with pioneer hill country life, outstanding mountain folk, remedies
used, and superstitions believed in this mountain area, as well as a rich
selection of folktales and legends. Occasional line drawings of native
mountain flowers add to the attractiveness of the work.

229   Roberts, Nancy.   *Ghosts of the Carolinas.*   McNally   (I, J)
      and Loftin, 1962.   62p.

> Perhaps they have forgotten that there are mysteries on our own
> planet still unsolved.

From the Gray Man of Pawley's Island to the Talking Corpse of
Old Salem Tavern, a host of ghosts and apparitions found in both Carolinas are explored in this most intriguing book. Eighteen short selections
describing the legends and tales of these mysteries are evenly shared
between the two states. Names of actual people who have experienced
these occurrences are provided in some selections, thereby adding to
the convincing nature of the stories. All kinds of ghosts are covered,
ranging from human ghosts to the Hound of Goshen and even the
Brown Mountain Lights. Possible scientific explanations are given when
possible or available. The author's husband, Bruce Roberts, has en-

hanced the appealing and captivating nature of the book with his art-
ful, attractive photographs of the sites of some of the stories.

230 Scott, Flo Hampton. *Ghosts with Southern Accents* (J, S)
     and Evidence of Extrasensory Perception. Illus.
     Southern Univ. Pr., 1969. 134p.

> . . . This book will not tell you that there are actually ghosts.

In clipped, straightforward sentences that do not wait for evalu-
ations of emotions or motives of ghosts or their hosts (a style admirably
suited to accounts of supernatural visitations), the author tells some
exciting stories she has heard near the Natchez Trace where she
lives. Alabama ghosts are included in the accounts.

231 Willis, Carrie Hunter, and Walker, Etta Belle. (J, S)
     Legends of the Skyline Drive and the Great Valley of op
     Virginia. Dietz Pr., 1937. 122p.

> . . . Where a native grass grew on which buffalo fattened and game
> lived all year.

In these loosely-connected stories of the early settlers we have a
view of the way they lived, the towns they established, and the richness
and roughness of their surroundings. The people in the valley were
German, Scotch-Irish, English, and Indian. Some of the tales were
gathered from early written accounts and from history books; others
are handed down by word-of-mouth. Illustrations are included, but not
a map, which would have been useful.

232 Windham, Kathryn Tucker. *Thirteen Georgia Ghosts* (I, J)
     and Jeffrey. Illus. by Frances Lanier. Strode, 1973.
     154p.

> Some noise had aroused him though, some unusual noise.

Hugh's discovery of the ghost collie on Scataway begins with that
unusual noise. Each of the thirteen ghost stories is a realistic tale of
the supernatural and is an interesting way of learning about some unusual places in Georgia. The reader will also gain insight into some of
the history and customs of the area.

233 Windham, Kathryn Tucker, and Figh, Margaret Gillis. (I, J, S)
     13 Alabama Ghosts and Jeffrey. Illus. Strode, 1969.
     120p.

> Frankly, until we saw the photograph of Jeffrey . . . we were skeptical
> about ghosts.

Thirteen ghost tales of Alabama are put into a collection in which
each is so absorbingly told that all age readers will thrill to the mysti-

cal events. *Jeffrey Introduces 13 More Southern Ghosts,* a later book by Kathryn T. Windham, gives a more detailed description of Jeffrey, the author's house-ghost. A photograph of Jeffrey and a friend is shown in the preface. Photography throughout the book is good, showing many Alabama homes and historical sites.

POETRY, DRAMA, MUSIC

234   Glass, Paul, and Singer, Louis C.   *Songs of Hill and*   (J, S)
      Mountain Folk: Ballads, Historical Songs.   Grosset,
      1967.   64p.

> We have sought to preserve the stylistic quality of the folk song for the enjoyment of all. . . .

Cecil Sharp visited the southern Appalachians in 1916 and 1917. He recorded 1,162 tunes representing 500 songs. While no one state can claim most of these songs, they are all typical of those sung in the mountaineer sections of Alabama. The songs are arranged for voice and piano with guitar chords. Simplified instructions on styling and strumming and a chart of basic guitar chords are included.

235   Green, Paul.   *The Common Glory.*   Univ. of North   (S)
      Carolina Pr., 1948.   273p.   (Reprint ed., Greenwood,
      1973)

> We must continue the struggle . . . against . . . the enemy of disunion, of selfishness, of greed.

The play opens at the beginning of the revolutionary war in April, 1775, and changes from the court of George III of England to the House of Burgesses in Williamsburg, then to the governor's palace, the battlefield at Yorktown, and, finally, to Richmond. Thomas Jefferson, the drafter of the Declaration of Independence, and Patrick Henry, Virginia's eloquent governor, figure prominently in the action. Throughout this story of discouragement and struggle Jefferson pursues his dream of a just and righteous society as the "common glory" of all men. The play is still performed at Williamsburg.

236   Harwell, Richard B.   *Confederate Music.*   Illus.   (J, S)
      Univ. of North Carolina Pr., 1950.   184p.

> This volume grew out of a desire to learn what music was published in the Confederacy.

Mobile, Alabama, is known to be the site of several publishers of sheet music during this historical period. The first section of the book gives the history, development, and words of the better-known songs. The second section gives an alphabetical listing of the titles of the songs, the publishers, dealers, and a rather comprehensive bibliography.

237   Henderson, Rosamon.   *The Epic: The Battle of*   (J, S)
      Horseshoe Bend.   Banner Pr., 1969.   unp.

> Where the flowing Tallapoosa
> Bends its course into a horseshoe.

An epic poem of the Battle of Horseshoe Bend gives a history of the Creek Tribe nation and the Spanish and French early settlers. A description of Andrew Jackson's leadership in the defeat of the Creeks and their leader, Menawa, is also included.

238   Jarrell, Randall.   *The Bat-Poet.*   Illus. by Maurice   (I, J)
      Sendak.   Macmillan, 1963.   43p.

> I've made the words like the mockingbirds . . . so you can tell what its like in the daytime.

Rejected by his fellow bats, little brown bat amuses himself by watching and listening to the other birds and animals in the forest. Eventually he learns to put his thoughts into word-songs, which he shares with the mocking bird, the squirrel, the chipmunk, and finally with his own family of bats. The author cleverly incorporates many descriptions of birds and animals of his native North Carolina in this amusing fantasy of forest life.

239   Joyner, Charles W.   *Folk Song in South Carolina.*   (S)
      (Tricentennial Booklet, Number 9)   Univ. of South
      Carolina Pr., 1971.   112p.

> Since they tell faithfully the Negro's innermost life, both intellectually and spiritually, they are the only true source of our history.

This book is a survey of the origin and development of South Carolina folk songs. It contains a representative sampling of songs and a brief listing of sources. It also explains the importance of folk music in South Carolina history, and notes how the life-styles of both the whites and blacks in the state affected its folk songs. In some instances the music is included.

240   Lanier, Sidney.   *Poems of Sidney Lanier.*   Ed. by   (J, S)
      Mary Lanier.   Scribner, 1916.   262p.   (Reprint ed.,   op
      Univ. of Georgia Pr., 1967)

> Out of the hills of Habersham,
> Down the valleys of Hall . . .

These are the opening lines of the lovely poem "Song of the Chattahoochee" by this famous and beloved Georgia poet. The volume contains ninety-six of his poems plus the Centennial Cantata. The introduction is a biographical memorial to Lanier who was born in Macon, Georgia, in 1842. His home is still standing and is among Macon's tourist attractions. The Lanier Oak, in Brunswick, on the marshes of Glynn, is another beautiful spot in Georgia, as are the hills (mountains) of Habersham and the valleys of Hall.

241 Pearson, James Larkin. *My Fingers and My Toes.* (I, J, S)
Ingram, 1971. 278p.

> But I take the beauty of all your hills
> And weave it into a splendid song
> To gladden the world as it moves along.

This complete collection of the poems of the poet laureate of North Carolina was compiled by Wilkes Community College, Wilkesboro, North Carolina. From the young age of four-and-one-half, James Larkin Pearson displayed a rare gift of poetic expression. This collection, autobiographical in scope, reflects his genius, beginning with poems written during his childhood. Using a variety of poetic forms, the poet spans the years from the end of the nineteenth century to the present, including descriptions of farm life in the mountains, folklore, dialect pieces, expressions of religious faith, humor, and satirical comment.

242 Plair, Sally. *Something to Shout About: Reflections* (I, J)
on the Gullah Spiritual. Illus. and sketchings by
Annie Lyle Viser. Molasses Lane Publishers, n.d.
71p.

> These songs are but the vocal expression of the simplicity of their faith and the sublimity of their long resignation.

The characteristics and peculiarities of these Gullah spirituals are explained in this well-researched book. The shouting, swaying, tapping of feet, and patting of hands are all a part of the rhythmic body movements which sometimes accompany the singing of the Gullah spirituals and which set them apart from other native music. Words and music are given for many of these spirituals often heard in the Low Country of South Carolina from Myrtle Beach to the Savannah River.

243 Rutledge, Archibald. *The Everlasting Light and* (J, S)
Other Poems. (S. Price Gilbert Contemporary Poetry
Series) Univ. of Georgia Pr., 1949. 119p.

So when he offered love, with it he gave
Fringed gentians, cool lobelias, columbines;

Love, death, honor, religion, and beauty are the primary themes of these romantic verses. They are embellished throughout by words and phrases depicting the beauty of nature in the South. Archibald Rutledge, former poet laureate of the state, incorporates into these simple poems the spirit of South Carolina's people.

BIOGRAPHY AND PERSONAL ACCOUNTS

244 Aaron, Henry. *Aaron.* Rev. ed. with Furman Bisher.   (J, S)
     Illus. Crowell, 1968. 228p.

   I keep repeating about the two dollars, two pairs of pants and two sandwiches.

   Henry Aaron tells his own story of success. Leaving Mobile, Alabama, at age seventeen to join the Indianapolis Clowns was a big step for him. This is the account of his progress in baseball from $50-a-week shortstop to $200,000-a-year superstar.

245 Alderman, Clifford Lindsey. *Osceola and the*   (J, S)
     Seminole Wars. Messner, 1973. 189p.

   The first thing the Seminoles at the council table asked for was food.

   This easy-to-read, comprehensive biography of the famous Seminole chief begins in Alabama where Billy Powell (later given the Indian name of Osceola) lived with his Creek Indian mother and white stepfather. Indian customs, encounters with white settlers and soldiers, slave problems, and, finally, the wars are portrayed in a factual but sympathetic fashion. After a poignant description of Osceola's deathbed scene, the author follows the Seminoles through further tribulations to their present residency in the Florida Everglades.

246 Anderson, La Vere. *Mary McLeod Bethune.* Illus.   (P, I)
     by William Hutchinson. (A Discovery Book)
     Garrard, 1976. 80p.

   Africans in America need teachers just as much as Africans in Africa.

   Mary McLeod Bethune, granddaughter of a slave, rather than serve as a missionary to Africa, dedicated her life to the education of black children in the United States. With only $1.50 in coins, a strong faith, and the help of many friends, she founded a school in Daytona, Florida, which has grown into a thriving institution, Bethune-Cookman

College. Mrs. Bethune also held responsible positions in the federal government during the administration of Franklin Roosevelt. Written with sympathy, this well-researched biography is fine inspirational reading for all children. Mrs. Bethune's portrait now hangs in the South Carolina state capitol in Columbia.

247   Anderson, William.   *Wild Man from Sugar Creek: the*   **(S)**
          Political Career of Eugene Talmadge.   Louisiana State
          Univ. Pr., 1975.   268p.

> . . . pilgrimage to pay homage to the strength behind his power, . . . the rural electorate.

Eugene Talmadge, father of the present Senator Herman Talmadge, knowing where and who his supporters were, calculated many of his actions, his dress, and speeches to appeal to the mythical little man, the have-nots, the orphans of rural life newly arrived in the towns and cities. His political career which lasted twenty years included four terms as Georgia's governor. This is an interesting biography of one of the state's most colorful political figures and is based mainly on interviews with living contemporaries. It captures the changes in the southern mind during the 1930s and recreates the struggle between a fiercely independent politician and the rapid change in a conservative land.

248   Aulaire, Ingri d', and Aulaire, Edgar Parin d'.   **(P, I)**
          George Washington.   Illus. by the authors.
          Doubleday, 1936.   60p.

> The little boy from the lone Virginia plantation had become the Father of His Country.

George Washington is shown growing up on a plantation in Virginia, playing games with his family, attending school, learning to ride, studying surveying and, as a man, taking part in the affairs of the Virginia colony and eventually becoming commander-in-chief of all the colonial troops fighting against the British. The story concludes when he becomes the first president of the United States. The many colorful, stylized lithographs make this an appealing, easy-to-read biography for children.

249   Aulaire, Ingri d', and Aulaire, Edgar Parin d'.   **(P, I)**
          Pocahontas.   Illus. by the authors.   Doubleday, 1946.
          44p.

> He gave her the name Pocahontas, which means the one who plays mostly.

Pocahontas's life, in this picture book, begins with her childhood in the deep dark woods of Virginia and ends with her meeting with the king and queen of England. The lithographs show the many details of

Indian life and add humor to the story of the Indian princess who saved John Smith's life and befriended the Jamestown colony.

250 Avant, D. A. *Like a Straight Pine Tree: Stories of*   (J, S)
     Reconstruction Days in Alabama and Florida 1885–
     1971. Illus. David A. Avant, Jr., 1971. 124p.

> Papa and I went once to Montgomery . . . and he bought a parlor organ.

In a nonchronological account of incidents in the life of Avant, an octogenarian, a realistic picture is given of life in Alabama and Florida during the years 1885-1971. The moral tone of the work exemplifies the upright character of this well-known man. The book takes its title from the hymn, "God Who Touchest Earth with Beauty."

251 Barrett, Marvin. *Meet Thomas Jefferson.* Illus. by   (P, I)
     Angelo Torres. (Step-up Books Series) Random,
     1967. 86p.

> "By these," he had written, "I wish most to be remembered!"

Thomas Jefferson was the author of the American Declaration of Independence, the Statute of Virginia for Religious Freedom, and father of the University of Virginia; but these were only a few of his accomplishments. Jefferson's life from birth to death is covered completely in this simple and interesting biography. He was a man of many talents who made great contributions to his country; each one is covered briefly.

252 Bigland, Eileen. *Helen Keller.* Illus. by Lili Cassel   (I, J)
     Wronker. S. C. Phillips, 1967. 192p.

> It was over nine years since Anne Mansfield Sullivan had begun her prodigious task of teaching Helen.

The life of Helen Keller is a legend, not only to the people of America but to the whole world. This story of Tuscumbia, Alabama, where Helen Keller was born, relates the major events of that life— darkness, the first words, learning to speak in more than one language, work at Radcliffe, lecture tours. The author's storytelling art makes the events come to life and entertains the intermediate reader.

253 Black, J. Gary. *My Friend the Gullah: A*   (J, S)
     Collection of Personal Experiences. Illus. by Nancy
     Ricker Webb. Beaufort Book Co., 1974. 50p.

> De crop bu'n up wid de dry drout? We ain't hab rain in mos' four week now.

For fifty years Gary Black served as the auditor for Beaufort County and learned Gullah, the unusual dialect spoken by the blacks of the Sea Islands. This book is a collection of stories about these people, told in the native dialect. An article on the Gullah by Dr. Julian K. Quattlebaum, Sr. adds greatly to the usefulness of the volume for students. Readers of *The Water is Wide* or *Conrack* by Pat Conray or *Sea Island Lady* by Francis Griswald will welcome the information on Daufuskie, St. Helena, and Hilton Head Islands.

254 Blackburn, Joyce. *James Edward Oglethorpe.* (I, J)
Lippincott, 1970. 144p.

Jamie knew the marchers were about to be outnumbered and halted by a crowd. . . .

The civil rights demonstration mentioned here occurred in the 1700s in England. James Oglethorpe dropped out of college, turned his back on the "comfortable life," and entered the political arena. In this extensively researched book, the author records not only the life of Oglethorpe but the founding of Georgia and the state's early history. The reproduction of a portrait of Oglethorpe and a map of the coastal section of Georgia assist the reader in understanding the man and the area.

255 Blackburn, Joyce. *Martha Berry: Little Woman with* (I, J)
a Big Dream. Lippincott, 1968. 158p.

Giving was not a duty; it was the natural way to live.

This was the way of life young Martha Berry learned from her adored father. Their way of giving was to help people help themselves. Starting with a tiny log cabin, Martha devoted her life to building a school where under-privileged children could be taught a vocation along with academic studies. Today visitors to Georgia can tour her home and the Berry Schools where young Americans still study to prepare themselves for a better life.

256 Blassingame, Wyatt. *Osceola, Seminole War Chief.* (I)
Illus. by Al Fiorentino. Garrard, 1967. 80p.

Suddenly he pulled a knife from his belt and stabbed it through the paper.

Thus did Osceola respond when the Seminoles were ordered by the army to leave their Florida lands for the unknown West. This well researched biography for younger readers tells of the resistance of the Seminole Indians to the federal orders to give up their lands and move to the West. Captured through trickery, Osceola was imprisoned at Fort Moultrie in Charleston Harbor where he died and was buried. Illustrations in two colors give a realistic picture of Indian tribal life.

257   Bussman, Marlo Pease.   *Born Charlestonian: the*   (J, S)
      Story of Elizabeth O'Neill Verner.   State Printing
      Co., 1969.   120p.

   The fact that you can catch more flies with honey than with vinegar
was the basis of Beth's success.

   Charleston's most famous artist, Elizabeth O'Neill Verner, is the
heroine of this short biography. Widowed, with two children to support, Beth Verner turned to art for a livelihood. Her works interpreted
the character of her beloved Charleston and its people, and she became
highly successful. It was said that she was an ambassador of goodwill
wherever she went. This beautiful book is illustrated with some of Mrs.
Verner's own lithographs.

258   Byers, Tracy.   *Martha Berry, the Sunday Lady of*   (S)
      Possum Trot.   Putnam, 1932.   268p.   (Reprint ed.,   op
      Gale, 1971)

   As she paused before a cabin where lived these people of proud
heritage. . . .

   These are the people Martha Berry came to know and love
through her father, Captain Berry. The land across the road from their
spacious home, deeded to Martha shortly before her father's death, was
where she established the Berry Schools. Martha traveled widely and
entertained many of the great of her day as she sought support for the
schools, which were established to educate and train poor mountain
boys and girls. A beautifully written biography of a truly great woman,
this story of her devotion to an ideal is simply and vividly told. It is
well illustrated with photographs.

259   Campbell, Norine Dickson.   *Patrick Henry: Patriot*   (S)
      and Statesman.   Devin-Adair, 1969.   437p.

   What, then, were the awakening excellencies of his genius—that magic
touch with which he drew men to him?

   From his first great speech, "The Parson's Cause," in 1763 to his
retirement in 1790 Patrick Henry was a central figure in helping to
bring about the break with England, and the Revolution, and in the
formation of the governments of Virginia and the newborn nation. He
was often opposed by strong aristocratic leaders who saw him as a
coarse, unlearned backwoodsman but they were forced to praise his
genius. A consistent characteristic throughout his varied career was his
courageous defense of man's right to freedom. With the use of documents, letters, biographies, and the writings of others the author attempts to seek the truth about Patrick Henry and to refute the writings
of those who were critical of him. The annotated bibliography and the

comprehensive index make this scholarly work especially valuable for the advanced student.

260 Campion, Nardi Reeder. *Patrick Henry: Firebrand* (I, J)
of the Revolution. Illus. by Victor Mays. Little,
1961. 261p.

His head was high. His deep-set eyes blazed. His rich voice sent chills through his listeners.

Patrick Henry—a friendly, carefree school dropout—decided after years of failure as a storekeeper and farmer to become a lawyer. With only a meager knowledge of law, but with daring and eloquence and great conviction regarding dignity and human rights, he challenged any opponent. His fiery speeches and his resolutions against the Stamp Act in the House of Burgesses in Williamsburg in May, 1765, sparked the beginning of resistance to the unfair British rule. Other great leaders and the events of the times are revealed through this recounting of Henry's life. An index and bibliography are included.

261 Clancy, Paul R. *Just a Country Lawyer.* Indiana (S)
Univ. Pr., 1974. 301p.

Sam Ervin tried to pass along the same love of truth and integrity that his father had drilled into him . . . by example.

This readable, objective biography of the North Carolina senator made famous by the Watergate hearings, traces his background from the early Scotch-Irish pioneer forefathers who gave him his passionate love of freedom to his recent retirement from public office. Chapters on his early life and teenage years in Morganton give a realistic picture of life in a small North Carolina town before World War I. A section of family photographs adds interest to this part of the biography. Later chapters recount his civil rights and human liberties activities. A comprehensive index makes the work useful for the serious student.

262 Commager, Henry Steele, and Ward, Lynd. (I)
America's Robert E. Lee. Illus. by Lynd Ward.
Houghton, 1951. 111p.

Lee was at once an American and a Virginian. . . . What should he do if Virginia seceded?

This portrait of Robert E. Lee gives a clear and impartial view of his life, his career, and his part in the Civil War. His choice to serve the Southern rather than the Union cause was one of the most difficult he ever had to make. A general account of the war, important battles, and Lee's leadership of the Confederate army are accurately and vividly described. The surrender, as recalled by a Union officer, is moving.

263 Cunliffe, Marcus. *George Washington and the* (I, J)
Making of a Nation. (American Heritage Junior
Library) American Heritage, 1966. 155p.

His life and the meaning of his life became as vast as the United
States itself.

Washington is much admired and respected. Many myths have
grown up around him, and it is difficult to dispel them and present a
realistic portrait of the man. While the book covers his entire life, it
emphasizes his life in Virginia before the war and his military leadership during the Revolution. The many prints, paintings, maps, and letters further enliven the text.

264 Daly, Robert Walter. *Raphael Semmes: Confederate* (J, S)
Admiral. Illus. by James J. Fox. Kenedy, 1965.
191p.

You worked wonders with that dull little sailer *Sumpter.* You'll dazzle
the world with the *Alabama.*

None could know that the *Alabama* in Semmes's hands was
destined to become the greatest commerce raider in naval history. The
author draws a portrait of an orphaned boy who at sixteen entered the
Navy. A veteran of the Mexican War, the biographee cast his lot with
the Confederacy when the South seceded. As commander of the Confederate steamship *Sumpter* and the *Alabama,* Semmes was the naval
hero of the South. Naval battles of the war between the states are
vividly depicted. Boys, especially, will thrill to the heroic image of
Semmes and the exciting battle scenes.

265 Daniels, Jonathan. *Mosby, Gray Ghost of the* (J)
Confederacy. Illus. by Albert Orbean. Lippincott,
1959. 122p.

No fighting man had ever been able to drive Mosby from the Virginia
country he loved.

Escaping from almost impossible situations, moving behind enemy
lines, and attacking enemy soldiers more numerous than his own,
Mosby seemed to lead a charmed life. Before the war was over there
was a price on his head. An insight into the tactics of guerilla warfare
and into the politics within a military force are portrayed in the details
of Mosby's actions during the Civil War.

266 Daniels, Jonathan. *Robert E. Lee.* Illus. by Robert (I, J)
Frankenburg. Houghton, 1960. 184p. op

Lee was defeated. Yet somehow the power of his dignity dominated
the scene when he rode . . . to surrender. . . .

Following Lee from his childhood through West Point and the Mexican War, the author concentrates on Lee's major role in the Civil War. His final years as president of Washington College in Lexington, where he hoped to educate a new generation to rebuild the South, are discussed. This tender but objective portrayal makes it evident why Lee, the great military hero, was loved and honored by both friend and foe.

267 Daniels, Jonathan. *Stonewall Jackson.* Illus. by (I, J)
William Moyers. (Landmark Series) Random, 1959.
183p.

> There is Jackson standing like a stone wall. Follow me!

General Jackson led his troops in battles that are now famous—Bull Run, Richmond, Chancellorsville. He believed in striking the enemy hard, fast, and where it hurt the most thereby bringing his men victory. In turn they trusted, loved, and followed him into battle. Although the book covers his early life as well as his military career, more attention is paid to the latter. His valley campaign is described in detail.

268 Daugherty, James. *Daniel Boone.* Original (I, J)
lithographs by the author. Viking, 1939. 95p.

> When they were through he knew the farms on the Yadkin would be safe again.

North Carolina played an important part in Boone's life for it was here the family moved from Kentucky: "Daniel stepped out from his boyhood into the kingdom of a man in a world almost as new as Genesis." From the Boone farm in the Yadkin Valley, he went out to fight with Captain Waddell and he returned here to his ever-growing family between westward hunting trips. The strong, compelling lithographs give life and excitement to the equally strong, descriptive prose of this biography for the teenage reader. The book's excellence was acknowledged when it was awarded the 1940 Newbery Medal.

269 Davidson, Margaret. *Helen Keller.* Illus. by Vicki (P)
Fox. Hastings, 1969. 94p.

> Helen's blind! She can't see. My baby's blind!

In adult life Helen is pictured as always busy, filling her days with fun and work. She is always ready to go to new places and try new things. This primary level book is simple enough to be a reader. Its central point is the incident in which Miss Keller understands W-A-T-E-R for the first time, although also related are stories of Helen's teacher-companion, college, and lecturing years.

270   Dial, Rebecca.   *True to His Colors: A Story of South*   (J, S)
Carolina's Senator Nathaniel Barksdale Dial.
Vantage, 1974.   200p.

I am fourteen, and I've got to be true to my colors!

These words were spoken by Senator Nathaniel Barksdale Dial, an ardent admirer, at an early age, of General Wade Hampton III. At fourteen, he proudly wore a "red shirt" in recognition of this loyalty to the general to whom concerned South Carolinians looked for leadership and deliverance during the Reconstruction era. Senator Dial, like General Hampton, concerned himself with the welfare of his people. He was responsible for most of the industrial improvements in the surrounding area. Senator Dial was a family man, lawyer, banker, businessman, and a United States senator. His lifetime spanned the post-Civil War era to the 1930s, a time of economic deprivation. This is a well-written, enjoyable biography which will especially appeal to teenagers.

271   Dillard, Annie.   *Pilgrim at Tinker Creek.*   Harper's   (S)
Magazine Pr., 1974.   217p.   (Paperback ed., Bantam,
1975)

On my right a woods thickly overgrown with creeper descended the hill's slope to Tinker Creek.

Widely acclaimed at the time of its publication, this personal narrative brings the reader anecdotes and odd pieces of information from experiences and explorations of the author during one year in and around her home in the Roanoke Valley of Virginia. She points out the sights and sounds around Tinker Creek: snakes, trees, and the woods leading to the Blue Ridge.

272   Eason, Jeanette.   *Leader by Destiny: George*   (J, S)
Washington, Man and Patriot.   Illus. by Jack Manley
Rose.   Harcourt, 1938.   402p.

"Thank God, sir, you are at the helm. So long as you stay there, we'll keep off the rocks!"

Whether standing before Congress pleading for peace, guiding the stormy tide of argument at the Constitutional Convention, riding among the troops at Princeton and Yorktown, sitting among the Burgesses at Williamsburg, or fighting the French and Indians with General Braddock in the wilderness, Washington was a leader. He helped shape the destiny of the country and the country in turn determined his. An index is included.

273 Edwards, Sally.   *The Man Who Said No.*   Coward,   (J, I)
     1970.   191p.

> Patriotism is a luxury we can ill afford.

This informal biography describes the life of James Louis Petigru, an unsophisticated farm boy who grew to be one of Charleston's
most prominent citizens. His life is traced from boyhood to Willington
Academy, one of America's first progressive schools; to the low-country
plantations; and to Charleston, the great social and cultural center of
the South. Petigru was an outstanding lawyer who stood alone in his
strong opposition to the secession of South Carolina from the Union
in 1860.

274 Egypt, Ophelia Settle.   *James Weldon Johnson.*   Illus.   (P, I)
     by Moneta Barnett.   Crowell, 1974.   41p.

> Soon the words came so fast James' fingers seemed to fly over the
> paper.

In the above fashion James Weldon Johnson wrote the words for
"Lift Every Voice and Sing," which black Americans came to regard
as their national song. Johnson (1871-1938) had a distinguished career
as poet, teacher, songwriter, attorney, diplomat, and civil rights leader.
He became the first black Secretary for the National Association for
the Advancement of Colored People. This brief biography concentrates
on his childhood education and early career in Florida, and especially
on his music and poetry. His later accomplishments are outlined
sketchily. The book is generously illustrated with drawings in color
which reinforce the narrative.

275 Einstein, Charles.   *Willie Mays: Coast to Coast Giant.*   (I, J)
     Putnam, 1963.   191p.

> The term spectacular is synonymous with Willie Mays. It's as simple
> as that.

Willie's grandfather was a semi-pro ball player in Tuscaloosa,
Alabama, around the turn of the century. His father also played baseball. At Fairfield Industrial High School, Willie played football and
basketball, but from an early age his real joy was playing baseball.
Throughout this story, the author tries to pinpoint what it is that gives
Mays the spark, the inspiration, the quickness that resulted in his outstanding success.

276 Felton, Harold W.   *James Weldon Johnson.*   Illus.   (I, J)
     by Charles Shaw.   Dodd, 1971.   91p.

> "A black person can do anything a white person can do," she said.

The above quotation was the advice of James Weldon Johnson's mother when he was growing up in Jacksonville, Florida. Johnson (1871-1938) took the advice and went on to a lifetime of successes as teacher, lawyer, editor, poet, songwriter, diplomat, politician, and civil rights advocate. He established the first high school for blacks in Jacksonville, and was the first black admitted to the Florida bar. This biographical sketch covers his entire career, with emphasis on his early accomplishments.

277 Fleming, Thomas J. *First in Their Hearts: a* (I, J)
Biography of George Washington. Norton, 1968. op
136p.

Yorktown brought Washington home to Virginia after six years of war.

Washington's return home did not last for, at age fifty-seven, he became the first president of the country. Again he found it necessary to leave his beloved Mount Vernon. This account of the life of Washington, which emphasizes his qualities of loyalty and judgment as well as his military ability, is at once personal and objective.

278 Foster, John. *Southern Frontiersman: The Story of* (I)
General Sam Dale. Illus. by Leslie Gray. Morrow,
1967. 191p.

For some years after the war, Dale operated a general store in what is now Monroe County, Alabama.

Known as "the Daniel Boone of Alabama," Sam Dale was one of the most outstanding of the American frontiersmen. Although a friend of the Indians, he fought with them in the settlement of the South. The accounts of his experiences with the Indians cover a fascinating and comparatively little known period of Alabama and southern history.

279 Frady, Marshall. *Wallace.* World, 1968. 246p. (J, S)

Born in a small crackerbox just outside Clio, Alabama. . . .

The life of George C. Wallace, from his birth in August 1919, to his campaign for the presidency of the United States, is told in a most informal manner. It covers his growing up, his years at the University of Alabama, his marriage to Lurleen, his wartime experiences, and his political activities. This is a readable biography with a great many human interest sidelights.

280 Freeman, Douglas Southall. *Lee of Virginia.* (J, S)
Scribner, 1958. 256p.

You will take with you the satisfaction that proceeds from the consciousness of duty faithfully performed.

In his last order to his troops Lee spoke these words, which, although they were meant for his army, especially represented his life. Lee faithfully performed whatever duties befell him, whether caring for his ailing mother, planning battle strategies, or acting as college president. The major part of this biography covers the Civil War years, however the emphasis is on the character of Lee rather than his military career. This book is a result of the extensive research done for the four-volume study of the life of Robert E. Lee. An index is included.

281   Fritz, Jean.   *Where was Patrick Henry on the 29th of*   (P)
          May?   Illus. by Margot Tomes.   Coward, 1975.
          47p.

On the 29th of May, what was he doing? . . . He was bawling out the King again.

All his life important things seemed to happen to Patrick Henry on the 29th of May. He was even born on the 29th of May. Failing as a planter and storekeeper, Patrick finally became a lawyer and began to use what people called his "sending voice." No matter where he was, he was likely to be orating; he especially liked to speak about freedom and rights. That is why on the 29th of May, 1765, he was "bawling out the King." Humorous drawings add to the story.

282   Goodrum, John C.   *Wernher von Braun: Space*   (J, S)
          Pioneer.   Illus.   Strode, 1969.   166p.

The fulfillment of von Braun's lifelong dream for a manned flight to the moon and back begins unfolding with the launch of Apollo II.

The life story of the great space scientist, who helped America become a preeminent spacefaring nation, begins in Berlin, Germany. With his associates and his family in Huntsville, Alabama, the work of designing and building a new rocket as well as a new life is begun. The appendix contains statements of Dr. von Braun's from his press conferences.

283   Graff, Steward, and Graff, Polly Anne.   *Helen Keller:*   (P, I)
          Toward the Light.   Illus. by Paul Frame.   Garrard,
          1965.   80p.

"I cannot stop to grow old while there is so much work to do," she said, "and so many children to help."

This simple portrayal of the life of Helen Keller, and her teacher, takes her through the years of growing up and into a very active and satisfying adult life. Beautiful color illustrations make this book with its simple vocabulary popular with upper primary or intermediate boys and girls.

284   Graham, Shirley. *Booker T. Washington: Educator*   (I, J)
   of Hand, Head and Heart. Messner, 1955. 192p.

    Teacher, wise helper of his race; good servant of God and country.

Born a slave, Booker T. Washington struggled for an education. He walked or worked his way five hundred miles to attend Hampton Institute. Later he was an instructor there. Believing his people needed the tools of freedom and to learn to work as a free people, he was commissioned at age twenty-two to found a college for blacks at Tuskegee, Alabama. The college produced teachers, carpenters, tinsmiths, and farmers. The struggle to build the college, from the time he borrowed the money to buy the land until Andrew Carnegie gave it a large endowment, was a very personal experience for this famous educator.

285   Graham, Shirley, and Lipscomb, George D. *Dr.*   (I, J)
   George Washington Carver, Scientist. Messner, 1944.
   248p.

    Start where you are, with what you have. Make something of it. Never be satisfied.

This famous black man, though born a slave, was able to put himself through Tuskegee Institute. Then he worked with the people and land around them, improving their diet as well as their economic level. He received many honors for the results of his creative research using clay, peanuts, sweet potatoes, cotton, and waste materials to make numerous useful products. This is a comprehensive biography.

286   Grant, Matthew G. *Osceola and the Seminole War.*   (P, I)
   Illus. by Harold Heriksen and John Keely. (Gallery of
   Great Americans Series) Childrens Pr., 1973. 31p.

    We will fight until the last drop of our blood sinks into these lands.

The Seminole Indians in Florida so successfully resisted the determined efforts of those who would dispossess them that today they still live in the Florida Everglades. Their leader, Osceola, was captured by trickery and imprisoned at Fort Moultrie in South Carolina, where he died and was buried. The author has used history as a background for a colorful story for young children. Beautifully illustrated in color and in black and white, this book will be especially useful with minority children in building a pride in their heritage.

287   Green, Margaret. *President of the Confederacy:*   (J, S)
        Jefferson Davis. Messner, 1962. 190p.

    On February 22, 1862, Jefferson Davis was officially inaugurated as President of the Confederacy.

Davis is portrayed as honorable even in defeat. His statesmanship, service in the U.S. military, and years in the Senate are recognized. Even his task of welding together the Confederate government is shown in an admirable light. A bibliography and index make this work a possible reference tool in the study of the Civil War, Jefferson Davis, and southern history in general.

288   Griffin, Judith Berry. *Nat Turner.* Illus. by Leo   (I, J)
        Carty. Coward, 1970. 62p.

    Nat talked about freedom—freedom for all the slaves.

When his father ran away to escape the bonds of slavery, Nat began to think about freedom. As Nat grew older he believed more and more that all men should be free. His beliefs led him to plan and carry out a rebellion to free the slaves. This sympathetic portrait of Nat Turner, which is dedicated to the theme of freedom, focuses on his early formative years and the forces which shaped his destiny.

289   Haley, Gail E. *Jack Jouett's Ride.* Viking, 1973.   (P)
        unp. (Paperback ed., Penguin, 1975)

    What he saw there froze his blood. It was Tarleton, "Bloody Tarleton". . . .

In 1781 Jack Jouett rode forty miles from Cuckoo to Charlottesville to warn Thomas Jefferson and other patriots that Tarleton and his Green Dragoons were coming to capture them. The author's linoleumblockprint illustrations capture the drama and setting of the event. The work provides excellent supplementary material for an elementary school unit on colonial America or the revolutionary war.

290   Harner, Charles E. *Florida's Promoters: The Men*   (J, S)
        Who Made It Big. Trend House, 1973. 72p.

    Until man came along and fixed it up, Florida was no place to live.

There were eight men and one woman who, between the Civil War and the Great Depression, did most of the fixing. They drained swamps, dredged up islands, built railroads and hotels, brought in tourists and settlers, established banks, made and lost fortunes, and literally created today's Florida. Their names were: Hamilton Disston, Henry Plant, Henry Flagler, Bion Barnett, Bertha Palmer, D. P. Davis, Barron Collier, Carl Fisher, and George Merrick. Here are their stories and accomplishments, briefly and entertainingly told and illustrated with contemporary photographs.

291   Hartley, William, and Hartley, Ellen. *Osceola, the*   (S)
     Unconquered Indian. Hawthorn, 1973. 293p.

"What I say I will do. Speak or not speak, what I resolve that will I execute."

The young Seminole warrior, Osceola, was addressing Indian Agent Thompson, expressing his peoples' determination to remain in Florida. War leader of the Seminoles during the Second Seminole War (1838-42), Osceola emerged as one of the great Indian leaders in American history. Never surrendering, finally captured through treachery, Osceola was respected even by his enemies. In this readable and well-researched biography, he comes to life both as a man and as a historical figure.

292   Henri, Florette. *George Mason of Virginia.* Ed. by   (J, S)
     Carolyn Tragger. Crowell-Collier, 1971. 182p.

"That all men are created equally free and independent," Mason's Virginia Declaration began. . . .

The derivation of the philosophy of democracy by Mason and other founding fathers is traced, and the sometimes selfish motives for breaking with Mother England are discussed. This is a well-written biography about a little-known Virginian.

293   Higginbotham, Don. *Daniel Morgan, Revolutionary*   (S)
     Rifleman. Univ. of North Carolina Pr., 1961. 239p.

Great generals are scarce—there are few Morgans to be found.

Although this book includes information about events of the revolutionary war, it is essentially about Daniel Morgan. His life is traced from about eighteen years of age through his last days. Though illiterate and uncultured, he combined the resourcefulness of the frontier with the native gift of leadership. Prior to the British invasion of the South, Morgan joined the Southern army; his experiences in two Indian wars provided him with tactics he could use in the revolutionary war. He saw heavy service in the Southern campaign, climaxing his military career at the Battle of Cowpens.

294   House, Jack. *Lady of Courage: The Story of Lurleen*   (S)
     Burns Wallace. League Press, 1969. 164p.

This great lady of our state embraced the three essential qualities necessary for greatness. . . .

A mother of four, Lurleen Wallace became the third woman to hold the office of governor of a state and the first in Alabama. When Lurleen Burns met her future husband, George Corley Wallace, in Tuscaloosa, he was attending the University of Alabama and she was working in the S. H. Kress "five and ten-cent" store. This is an inspiring story for all ages.

295 Huie, William Bradford. *He Slew the Dreamer.*   (J, S)
Delacorte, 1970. 260p.

> Through all those hours of testimony Ray appeared to enjoy himself and to grow stronger as the rest of us grew weary.

William B. Huie brings into print a masterful story of James Earl Ray's life, motives, and activities, tracing from the beginning one of the most shocking and publicized cases of assassination in the United States, the murder of Martin Luther King. The appendix includes a few of the many letters received by Ray during his time in the Shelby County jail.

296 Jackson, Robert E. *Joe Namath, Superstar.* Illus.   (I, J)
Walck, 1968. 48p.

> He is not only the best athlete I've ever coached, but the best athlete I've ever seen.

A readable biography of Namath portrays him as having close family ties, being especially considerate of his mother. He is essentially friendly, modest, and very likeable in spite of his public image. From a very successful university football career he goes into professional ball, where his large contracts reveal the success of this man whose beginnings seemed hampered by poverty.

297 Judson, Clara Ingram. *George Washington: Leader of*   (I)
the People. Illus. by Robert Frankenberg. Follett,   op
1951. 224p.

> Until this momentous moment, the people had not needed the kind of leader he was to become.

Washington left his home in Virginia three times to serve his country. Seeking adventure he joined Braddock to fight the French and Indians in the wilderness; then his fellow countrymen sought him out—first, to lead their army against the British in the Revolution, and then to lead the nation as President. Many dramatic scenes which are historically accurate are used to enliven the text. When possible the actual spoken words are used, but when no records were available, words and phrases from letters, diaries, and newspapers of the time are used.

298   Judson, Clara Ingram.   *Soldier Doctor: The Story of*   (P, I)
          William Gorgas.   Illus. by Robert Doremus.
          Scribner, 1942.   151p.

"A real soldier," Willie said the words over proudly as he dashed down the stairs for more water.

The emphasis of the story is Gorgas's army career. Every man in the Sanitary Corps loved him and would have done anything he asked. Simple vocabulary, large print, and busy pictures make the book especially suitable for upper primaries. There is a listing of Gorgas's earned honors, a type of entry that seems to delight this age reader.

299   Judson, Clara Ingram.   *Thomas Jefferson: Champion*   (I, J)
          of the People.   Illus. by Robert Frankenberg.   op
          Follett, 1952.   224p.

For the support of this declaration, we mutually pledge . . . our lives . . . and our sacred honor.

Thomas Jefferson was willing to give everything—his life, his land, his fortune. He believed so strongly in freedom and the rights of man that he met the challenges presented him and in so doing became the champion of the common people. In this well researched biography Jefferson appears as a contemporary spirit; the author has accomplished her purpose of bringing to life his philosophy of government, his ideal of freedom, and his faith in man.

300   Krementz, Jill.   *Sweet Pea: A Black-girl Growing Up*   (P, I)
          in the Rural South.   Illus.   Harcourt, 1969.   94p.   op

I don't know where I got the name Sweet Pea.

Sweet Pea talks about her family and friends, her school and church, and how she spends her time. The photographs help to give an insight into a cultural pattern of life in the area of Montgomery, Alabama. The foreword is written by Margaret Mead.

301   Lachicotte, Alberta.   *Rebel Senator: Strom*   (S)
          Thurmond.   Devin-Adair, 1966.   225p.

Once he sets his mind about something, nothing on earth can change it.

Strom Thurmond's political life and beliefs are vividly portrayed in this account of the years from his governorship of South Carolina and his write-in election to the U.S. Senate, through his embracing the Republican Party and backing Barry Goldwater for the Presidency. The influence of his young bride on his life and thinking was very pronounced. Jean Thurmond could quickly and quietly size up a person then ask the senator the searching questions which would enable him to assess the situation. Anyone interested in politics or government will find this readable and factually accurate book a welcome addition to a private collection or as background for today's politics.

302   Libby, Bill.   *Ken Stabler, Southpaw Passer.*   Illus.   (J, S)
      Putnam, 1977.   128p.

      And the Bear called Stabler the greatest quarterback he ever coached.

Ken Stabler led the Crimson Tide of Alabama to a Bowl victory and a national championship. From Foley, Alabama, to the Oakland Raiders was a rocky road for this left-handed passer, but his story is exciting and inspirational.

303   Lisitsky, Gene.   *Thomas Jefferson.*   Viking, 1935.   (J, S)
      358p.   op

      It is surprising how much you can do if you are always up and doing.

Jefferson was always up and doing; a man of varied talents, he made many contributions to the new country. Detailed discussions of Jefferson's philosophical and political ideas, including his dreams of education for everyone and his solution to the slavery problem, are found in this biography which idealizes the man, rarely treating his faults but rather unfairly presenting those of his opposition. Descriptions of colonial life in the colonies, especially Virginia, and of Jefferson's activities in France are excellent. Many quotations from contemporary accounts appear. A bibliography and thorough index are included.

304   Longsworth, Polly.   *I, Charlotte Fortem, Black and*   (I, J)
      Free.   Crowell, 1970.   248p.

      From the moment I heard about Port Royal, I wanted to go there.

Based on a journal kept by Charlotte Fortem, this biography tells the story of her teenage years spent in Salem, Massachusetts. She later came to South Carolina as a teacher in the Port Royal experiment, a federally funded plan for educating the freed slaves. Other notables mentioned are William Lloyd Garrison, William Wells Brown, Lucretia Mott, Frederick Douglass, and Harriet Tubman. An index makes this a useful reference work.

305   Marks, Henry S.   *Who Was Who in Alabama.*   (J, S)
      Strode, 1972.   200p.

      A permanent one-volume biographical record of outstanding residents of Alabama who have passed away.

The volume is arranged alphabetically and contains almost one thousand names of people from all walks of life who were leaders in the state. The short biographical sketches give students basic information about many Alabama residents who are not listed in more comprehensive reference tools.

306 Martin, Patricia Miles. *Dolley Madison.* Illus. by   (P)
    Unada. (A See and Read–Beginning to Read   op
    Biography) Putnam, 1967. 62p.

    Thee must wear not bright colors . . . And thee must remember to walk, not run.

Dolley Payne was brought up a Quaker, first in Virginia and then in Philadelphia. If she wished to break away from her Quaker garb and wear bright clothes as a girl, she had her chance to do so as a woman. She married James Madison, the great Virginia statesman and moved to his plantation, Montpelier, in Virginia. When he was elected president, Dolley became the first lady of the land. The story is written with an understanding of Quaker beliefs, and the historical background is simply but adequately portrayed.

307 Martin, Patricia Miles. *Pocahontas.* Illus. by Portia   (P)
    Takakjian. (A See and Read–Beginning to Read
    Biography). Putnam, 1964. 63p.

    Pocahontas begged that he not be killed and her father listened.

One of America's favorite heroines, Pocahontas, who rescued Captain John Smith from death, is depicted as the brave intelligent girl she was. This simple but vivid recounting of the settlement at Jamestown and its relationships with Powhatan's tribe emphasizes Pocahontas's desire for friendship with the colonists.

308 Meriwether, Louise. *Don't Ride the Bus on Monday:*   (I)
    The Rosa Parks Story. Illus. by David Scott Brown.
    Prentice-Hall, 1973. unp.

    Rosa Parks says of herself, "I'm just an average citizen."

The life story of Rosa Parks, who led the way in the civil rights movement in America gives her background and some of her personal experiences and those of family and friends during the 381 days of the bus boycott in Montgomery, Alabama.

309 Meriwether, Louise. *The Freedom Ship of Robert*   (P)
    Smalls. Illus. by Lee Jack Morton. Prentice-Hall,
    1971. 32p.

    Be sassy with your work, but not with your tongue.

This was the advice given Robert Smalls by his mother when he left his home in Beaufort to work for his freedom in Charleston. He captured a Confederate gunboat, the *Planter,* and carried fifteen other slaves to freedom during the Civil War. The pictures and maps throughout the book make this brief biography appealing to younger children.

310 Milverstedt, F. M. *The Quiet Legend: Henry Aaron.* (I, J)
Illus. Raintree, 1975. 47p.

> Progress . . . comes from the ability to learn.

The story of Henry (Hank) Aaron's climb to fame as a baseball player is woven into a strong character study of the man himself. Born into a poor, black family in Mobile, Alabama, he left home at seventeen to begin a fantastic career in professional baseball. Photos by Heins Fluetmeier add to the interest of the text.

311 Morse, Charles, and Morse, Ann. *Arthur Ashe.* (P, I)
Illus. by Harold Henriksen. (Creative Education
Books, Superstars) Children's Pr. for Amecus Street,
1974. 31p.

> Arthur was the first person out on the courts every day and the last to leave at night.

Arthur Ashe worked hard to become a good tennis player. With the help of his father and his coach, Dr. Johnson, he was launched into a game that at the time was dominated by white players. A major portion of the book deals with Ashe's life in Richmond, where he learned the game, and with his training with Dr. Johnson in Lynchburg. A certain vitality and honesty permeates the story.

312 Moscow, Henry. *Thomas Jefferson and His World.* (I, J)
(American Heritage Junior Library) American op
Heritage, 1960. 153p.

> Almost everything he tackled he improved.

Jefferson's interests were many and varied; his accomplishments were great. From history books we know he was a statesman, a legislator, and a diplomat. But do we know that he was also an architect, an inventor, a natural historian, a scientist, an agrarian, an intellectual, a humanitarian, and a patron of education and the arts? He contributed much to the world he lived in; his many talents and interests earned him the title "The sage of Monticello." This biography not only explores, through text and pictures, things he did in his life; it also interprets Jefferson, the man, and his times.

313   Nolan, Jeannette Covert.   *Yankee Spy, Elizabeth Van*   (I, J)
      Lew. (Biography Series)   Messner, 1970.   190p.

>   If I should ever have the chance to help the Union, I will.

Elizabeth Van Lew, a wealthy Richmond lady, spied for the Union under the noses of the leaders of the Confederacy for the ideals she believed in: that slavery be abolished and the Union be preserved. After the battle of Manassas, Union prisoners were brought to Richmond, and Elizabeth visited them taking food, blankets, and medicine. She aided in their escapes and served as a vital link in the underground network that existed throughout the South. A well-researched book that covers Elizabeth's spying activities from the fall of Fort Sumter to the fall of Richmond.

314   Radford, Ruby L.   *Juliette Low: Girl Scout Founder.*   (I)
      Illus. by Vic Dowd.   Garrard, 1965.   80p.

>   The Low family often came from England to their beautiful home LaFayette Square. . . .

The story of Juliette Low is also a story of growing up in earlier times in Savannah, Georgia. Juliette, or Daisy as she was called, was a warm, friendly girl, who grew up to be a woman with a great desire to be useful and to help others. Throughout her life she endeavored to live up to the promise and laws of the organization she founded. She not only worked for American girls but also for scouting and guiding all over the world.

315   Radford, Ruby L.   *Sequoya.*   Illus. by Unada.   (P)
      Putnam, 1969.   59p.

>   Wise medicine men say that lame people can sometimes work great magic.

This simple biography of Sequoya describes his early life when he was not able to run and play ball with his friends. It also tells of the wonderful gift he gave his people when he developed an alphabet for his tribe, the Cherokees, and helped them learn to read.

316   Randall, Ruth Painter.   *I Varina:* . . . .   Illus.   Little,   (J, S)
      1962.   243p.

>   Jeff says your health is better than he ever saw it. He thinks you now the finest woman he knows.

The biography of the girl who married Jefferson Davis and became the First Lady of the South is exciting and readable. Despite their differences in age, religion, and politics, the Davises rear six children and enjoy a happy life until the Civil War. After that the president of the Confederacy and his wife flee to Canada and later move back to a home on the Gulf in Mississippi.

317 Robertson, Ben. *Red Hills and Cotton: an Upcountry*   (S)
    Memory. Univ. of South Carolina Pr., 1960. 296p.

> My mind wanders all the time back to the lovely Keowee Valley.

Journalist Ben Robertson's deep feeling for the land and the people of his childhood is portrayed through his intimate style on each page of this biographical work. The people and the country taught Robertson to understand the past, to accept the present, and to hope for the future. He describes the people of the South as they work and play in everyday life, always taking time to live fully. A seventeen-page biographical sketch of Robertson by Wright Bryan adds perspective to Robertson's own story.

318 Sayers, John W., comp. *Who's Who in Alabama.*   (J, S)
    Vol. II. Sayers Enterprise, 1969. 520p.

> We know of no other source where you can have so much information on living Alabama individuals at your fingertips. . . .

This alphabetical listing of people who have done something outstanding in Alabama, or who have been elected to public office in the state is published independently. No one can pay their way in or buy a listing. A brief entry gives important facts and dates about each individual listed. A valuable reference tool for the secondary school.

319 Sloan, Steve. *Calling Life's Signals: The Steve Sloan*   (J, S)
    Story. Zondervan, 1967. 143p.

> Billy Graham said, "I remember Steve Sloan best as one of the leaders of the Fellowship of Christian Athletes."

Written by Sloan, with James C. Hefby's assistance, this story of his early life and his commitment to Christian leadership is most inspiring. The introduction by Paul W. (Bear) Bryant, Athletic Director and Head Football Coach at the University of Alabama, adds much to the veracity of the account.

320 Smiley, Nixon. *Crowder Tales.* Illus. by Quin Hall.   (J, S)
    Seamann, 1973. 169p.

> The women of Crowder were embarrassed if their husbands and children were not robust.

The author was one of those children in Crowder, a farming community near the Florida-Georgia line. An abundance of rich country food is one of the boyhood recollections which are the basis for these twenty-six brief stories originally published in the *Miami Herald.* Entwined with a small boy's adventures and misadventures is a fascinating cast of family, friends, and acquaintances. Their joys, sorrows, and eccentricities sketch a colorful picture of everyday life in the rural deep South during the years following World War I.

321   Smith, Bradford. *Captain John Smith: His Life and*   (J, S)
      Legend. Lippincott, 1953. 375p.   op

    No figure in American history has raised such a ruckus among scholars as Captain John Smith.

Smith has been doubted, called a liar, an imposter, a braggart, and even a villain by some scholars. This is due in part to the contents of his own writings, which seem at times incredible and contradictory. By others he is esteemed as a legendary hero and a saint. This is a most complete profile of the man, as well as an exciting adventure story. Because the author has done extensive research into his subject, Captain John Smith emerges a true historical figure. A list of sources and an index are included.

322   Smith, Ken. *The Willie Mays Story.* Illus.   (J, S)
      Greenberg, 1954. 94p.

    Free and easy, without a worry, the daily ball game is a romp to him. His confidence is boundless, his talent native.

An excellent sports story as well as an important addition to every black American collection, this account of Fairfield-born Willie Mays is beautifully illustrated with photographs. The foreword, by Leo Durocher, is another plus for the work.

323   Snow, Dorothea J. *Raphael Semmes: Tidewater Boy.*   (P, I)
      Illus. by Paul Laune. Bobbs-Merrill, 1952. 92p.

    Semmes of the *Alabama* was one of the distinguished heroes of the South, feared in war and respected in peace.

This easy-to-read biography recounts Semmes declaration of loyalty to his adopted state of Alabama during the Civil War. The book describes the way in which his skill and training aided the Confederacy as he became the feared enemy of Northern shipping, making his cruiser, the *Alabama,* the most daring raider on the seas.

324   Sobol, Donald J. *The Wright Brothers at Kitty*   (I, J)
      Hawk. Nelson, 1961. 143p.

    Kitty Hawk was a settlement of hardly two dozen poorly built houses scattered on a narrow strip of land.

Kitty Hawk, North Carolina, was so little known when Wilbur Wright first arrived there that even the local ship captains were unfamiliar with it. But to the Wright Brothers of Dayton, Ohio, it had just what they needed to test their glider: soft sand, sloping dunes, and, most important, a steady wind. This account of the development of the first heavier-than-air craft is told in a clear, factual manner that is easy to read and will appeal to young readers.

325 Spratt, Barnett. *Miss Betty of Bonnet Rock School,*   (I, J, S)
          1864-1865. Illus. by Joan Balfour Payne. Hastings,
          1963. 125p.

There was excitement at school today when the roof caught fire from sparks from the chimney.

Elizabeth Killian taught during the last year of the Civil War in a log schoolhouse in Chester County, South Carolina. Although she lacked books and other materials, the seventeen-year-old schoolmistress was both resourceful and courageous in her efforts to teach her young students. Her spare time was spent in knitting, rolling bandages, nursing wounded soldiers from both the Union and Confederate armies, and keeping this diary in which she recorded her love for a young soldier. It is reminiscent of Johanna Reiss' *The Upstairs Room* in its portrayal of homelife during wartime.

326 Starr, Bart, with Cox, Max. *Bart Starr*   (J, S)
          Quarterbacking. Prentice-Hall, 1967. 206p.

My life story is football . . . I honestly feel football is the finest sport in the world today.

Football is Bart Starr's world and he has won many honors in his chosen field. His place with the Green Bay Packers is an important factor in that team's record of victories. He recounts something of his problems, his pleasures, and the things that motivated him in becoming the number one quarterback in professional football. His team philosophy is one of the many facets of his character that has contributed to his greatness as a player, as a leader, and as a solid citizen.

327 Steele, William O. *Surgeon Trader, Indian Chief,*   (I, J)
          Henry Woodward of Carolina. Illus. by Hout
          Simmons. Sandlapper Pr., 1972. 96p.

The Englishman stood in the hot sands of a Carolina beach, surrounded by naked Cusabo.

Henry Woodward, a young surgeon, had volunteered to live among the Indian tribes for ten months and learn their customs and language. Although very little is known about Henry Woodward, the author of this short biography has used his facts to advantage in a readable version for young people. The book contains interesting facts about the early Indian tribes, rivalry between friendly and warring tribes, and competition between the English and the Spanish in the New World.

328   Sterne, Emma Gelders.   *Mary McLeod Bethune.*   (J, S)
Illus. by Raymond Lufkin.   Knopf, 1957.   268p.

To the day of her death, Mary McLeod Bethune proclaimed her pride in being African.

Granddaughter of a slave, Mary Bethune was steeped in the traditions of her African ancestors. But she was also proud of being an American. Through improving educational opportunities for youth, she hoped to change the status of blacks—especially black women. Founder of a successful college in Florida, member of the Executive Board of the National Urban League, on the Advisory Board of the National Youth Administration, and a special civilian assistant in the War Department, she made every effort to free her people from their bondage of prejudice and ignorance. The well-researched biography has an index.

329   Stevenson, Augusta.   *Booker T. Washington:*   (P, I)
Ambitious Boy.   Illus.   Bobbs-Merrill, 1960.   200p.

. . . Headlines in big black capital letters, one-inch high: PROFESSOR BOOKER T. WASHINGTON SPEAKS TONIGHT.

This story of Washington's birth into slavery, and his climb from plantation life and coal mining to the leadership of a renowned black training school is told in terms that a child can understand. The emphasis is on the childhood and thoughts of this famous black educator.

330   Stevenson, Augusta.   *Virginia Dare: Mystery Girl.*   (P, I)
Illus. by Harry Hanson Lees.   (Childhood of Famous
Americans Series)   Bobbs-Merrill, 1957.   192p.

In dugouts the Indians had come down that river and across the wide sound.

What happened to Virginia Dare, famous baby of the Lost Colony of Roanoke Island? No one really knows, but the author has woven an exciting adventure story around the few facts that have come to light through the years. Indian life of the colonial period is described in an easy-to-read style which should interest third and fourth graders. Simple line drawings add flavor to the text.

331   Syme, Ronald. *John Smith of Virginia.*   Illus. by   (I, J)
      William Stobbs.   Morrow, 1954.   192p.

   "I am held by the Indians," Smith wrote on the page.

When John Smith could not make friends with the Indians he outwitted them instead. A soldier, explorer, mapmaker, and prolific writer, John Smith was most of all a leader. By his own will he forced the men of the Jamestown Colony to survive in this wild and dangerous land. This is a realistic and exciting portrait of John Smith and the first permanent English settlement in the New World.

332   Syme, Ronald. *Osceola: Seminole Leader.*   Illus. by   (I, J)
      Ben F. Stahl.   Morrow, 1976.   96p.

   "I shall not leave this country, which has been my home since I was a child."

Born in northern Georgia to an English father and a Creek Indian mother, "Asi-Yahola" lived among white settlers until the end of the War of 1812 when, deserted by his white father, he and his mother fled to join other Creeks (now known as Seminoles) in northern Florida. Reasons for the conflict between Indians and settlers are given in a simple but unbiased text. Asi-Yahola, now known as Osceola, left his mother in the Tampa Bay area and moved on to become a Seminole leader during the wars with the white men, who tried to force the Indians to resettle west of the Mississippi River. Captured while negotiating under a flag of truce, he died in prison in 1838; but some of his followers fought on in the southern Florida swamplands where their descendants still live. Black-and-white illustrations, a one-page bibliography, and an in-depth index make this a worthwhile reference book for young readers.

333   Underwood, John. *Bear, The Hard Life and Good*   (J, S)
      Times of Alabama's Coach Bryant.   Illus.   Little,
      1974.   342p.

   What we're talking about here, really is motivating people, the ingredient that separates winners from losers. . . .

Bryant's philosophy of life is clearly stated in this account of his life from his childhood in a family of nine children to his successful career at the University of Alabama as head football coach and athletic director.

334   Vance, Marguerite. *Martha, Daughter of Virginia:*   (I)
      The Story of Martha Washington.   Illus. by Nedda   op
      Walker.   Dutton, 1946.   190p.

To her, it has been said, should go much credit for the winning of the war.

The story begins with a celebration of Martha Dandridge's eleventh birthday, when she remarks to her father that she would never be the "first" of anything, and ends when she becomes the First Lady of the United States. History, biography, and romance have been skillfully combined to re-create this pleasant picture of the life of Martha Washington.

335   Wallace, Cornelia.   *C'Nelia.*   Illus.   Lippincott,   (S)
      1976.   240p.

> The road to recovery is not smooth. It is like a jagged line on a stock market report.

The life story of Cornelia Wallace, subtitled "An Intimate Self-Portrait," takes her from childhood, where she grew up in the Alabama governor's mansion while her mother was official hostess for Governor Jim Folsom, through her marriage to Governor George Wallace. As the second wife of the governor times were not always pleasant. Some coverage is given to the telling of their difficult adjustment at the time of Wallace's injury and paralysis.

336   Wallace, George.   *Stand Up for America.*   Illus.   (J, S)
      Doubleday, 1976.   179p.

> If my message to my fellow citizens were to be summed up in a single phrase, it would be: Let's stand up for America.

This is a highly personal, intimate, and yet intensely political autobiography of George C. Wallace, governor of Alabama. He tells of his growing-up years, his university days, and his time as a flight engineer in the Pacific. Woven into this story is his romance with Lurleen Burns, who became his first wife and later was elected governor of Alabama. Finally, he tells why he will not give up despite physical and political limitations.

337   Wallace, George, Jr.   *The Wallaces of Alabama: My*   (J, S)
      Family.   Follett, 1975.   256p.

> I had a beautiful mother and I have an outstanding father, and who could ask for more?

Impelled by the tragic death of his mother, Lurleen, the attempt on his father's life which ended in such an ill-fated way, and his now narrow escape from drowning at the age of twenty-one, George Wallace, Jr. tells his very moving story to James Gregory, who assisted in preparing it for publication. George, Jr. gives a heartwarming account of what it was like to grow up as a member of one of the most famous political families in the modern South. An introduction by Governor George C. Wallace sets the tone of the work.

338   Walser, Richard.   *The Black Poet: The Story of*   (S)
George Moses Horton—A North Carolina Slave.
Philosophical Library, 1966.   120p.

> Must I dwell in slavery's night
> And all pleasure take its flight
> Far beyond my feeble sight
> Forever?

George Moses Horton was born in Northhampton County, North Carolina, just before the turn of the century. He was one of eight slaves belonging to William Horton, tavern-keeper and tobacco farmer. About 1800 the family moved to Chatham County. In middle age, George Moses Horton wrote a short, very high-sounding rhetorical autobiography which Walser has used as the framework for his work, which takes the poet's life from childhood to his death. Especially interesting are the passages describing George Moses Horton's relationships with students at the newly-established University of North Carolina at Chapel Hill. Poems included range from religious stanzas to odes for freedom. The work is indexed; notes and sources are listed in the final chapter.

339   Walser, Richard.   *Young Readers' Picture Book of Tar*   (J)
Heel Authors.   4th ed.   North Carolina Dept. of
Cultural Resources, 1975.   unp.

> [It was] prepared to help young readers . . . get better acquainted with North Carolina books and authors.

One-page essays, with photographs, give readable accounts of the lives and writings of some seventy writers who either lived in or wrote about North Carolina. The first eleven authors provide a historical perspective. The other authors represent writers best known to school age readers.

340   Walters, Helen B.   *Wernher von Braun: Rocket*   (J, S)
Engineer.   Macmillan, 1964.   185p.

> Youth of today faces an exciting future, bright with promise.

Compiled largely of quotes from von Braun himself, this story of his life in Germany and in America flows well through the many quotations. The photographs in themselves give an account of his life. Located in one signature at the front of the book, the pictures are a quick flip-through and preview of the larger work.

341 Washington, Booker T. *Up From Slavery: an*   **(J, S)**
Autobiography. (Great Illustrated Classics)
Doubleday, 1901. 230p.

Cast down your bucket where you are.

Booker T. Washington was born a slave in Franklin County,
Virginia. He describes his early life as a slave, which led to his ob-
session for an education. Dedicating his entire life to educating himself
and others, he founded Tuskegee Institute in Alabama. His speaking
efforts to raise money for that school led to his recognition as the first
of his race to become a noted public speaker. The book relates episodes of his life in both Alabama and Virginia. A section of photographs
is included.

342 Wibberley, Leonard. *Man of Liberty.* Farrar, 1968.   **(J, S)**
404p.

"Can a man asked to serve his country refuse with a good conscience..."

No history of this country can be complete without looking at
Jefferson since the concepts which he championed are basic to our form
of government and our national spirit. The author attempts to tell the
full story of Jefferson, depicting him as father, farmer, statesman and
scholar. The account is divided into four chronological sections: 1743–76,
1776–89, 1789–1801, 1801–26. For those who are interested in the story of
Jefferson's life in some breadth and something of the times in which he
lived, this biography, originally in four volumes, is a good choice. An
index is included.

343 Wilkinson, J. Harvie, III. *Harry Byrd and the*   **(S)**
Changing Face of Virginia Politics, 1945–1966.
Univ. Pr. of Virginia, 1968. 403p.

History values men as much for what they are as for what they
espouse.

This is a detailed study of the Byrd political machine and its
founder and "boss," Harry Flood Byrd, Sr. In it the organization of
Virginia politics around country courthouse cliques, the attitude toward
expenditures by the state, golden silence, and other Virginia political
phenomena are examined. It will interest mainly those who have a
distinct interest in Virginia politics.

344 William, Beryl, and Epstein, Samuel. *William*   **(I, J)**
*Crawford Gorgas: Tropic Fever Fighte*r. Illus. by
Robert Burns. Messner, 1953. 184p.

"There's a way I can get into the army after all!" Will said. "I can become an army doctor!"

A little boy born in Mobile, Alabama, grows up to become a man famous for his successful efforts against malaria in both Cuba and the Canal Zone. In story-like style, the authors tell of Gorgas's years as Surgeon General with the U.S. Army and of his retirement years, during which he was hailed as "Doctor of the World."

345 Wilson, Hazel.   *The Years Between: Washington at*   (I, J)
Home at Mount Vernon, 1783–1789.   Knopf, 1969.   op
148p.

"I am become a private citizen on the banks of the Potomac . . . free from the busy scenes of public life. . . . "

The years between Yorktown and the presidency were spent by Washington working to make Mount Vernon a prosperous estate. Based on daily entries in his diary and on his letters, this view of Washington reveals him as a man interested in every aspect of farming and devoted to his family, friends, and country.

OTHER INFORMATIONAL BOOKS

346 Akens, Helen Morgan, and Brown, Virginia Pounds.   (I, J)
Alabama Mounds To Missiles.   Illus.   Strode, 1962.
196p.

"Just what I want," exclaimed Wright. "I need room for a big field . . . and this is it."

In an entertaining and completely absorbing story of Alabama from the time of the first cave dwellers to the present, activities from head-flattening among the Indians to Wilbur Wright's flying school in Montgomery are described. The habits, peculiarities, regional trends, and common heritages are woven into the story. Geographical regions are shown in their relationship to each other and to the development of the state. It is well illustrated and very readable.

347 Anderson, Sherwood.   *The Buck Fever Papers.*   Ed.   (J, S)
by Welford Dunaway Taylor.   Univ. of Virginia Pr.,
1971.   250p.

The opening of . . . hunting season . . . saw Marion with a host of its best citizens missing. . . .

Buck Fever was the name Maxwell Anderson used for the fictitious reporter who contributed a series of whimsical stories to the two newspapers he owned in Marion, Virginia, in the late 1920s. Buck's comments on political and social mores made him more real than imaginary to readers of Anderson's newspapers. This is the first complete collection of the *Buck Fever* columns, and it provides a welcome excursion into a simple and humorous form of journalism that has virtually disappeared.

348   Atlanta Journal-Constitution. *Georgia Rivers.* Ed.   (J, S)
        by George Hatcher.   Univ. of Georgia Pr., 1962.   76p.

In her wild old days, the Savannah River ran red with mud and blood....

So begins the first article in this collection which was first published as a series in the *Atlanta Journal and Constitution Magazine.* All of the articles are beautifully written and illustrated with photographs and maps. In telling the stories of the state's rivers, the authors tell the story of Georgia, since the rivers have played a significant role in the state's development.

349   Bailey, Bernadine. *Picture Book of Florida.*   Rev.   (P, I)
        ed.   Illus. by Kurt Wiese.   Whitman, 1966.   32p.

The northern section is at its loveliest in spring when the azaleas, dogwood and magnolia are blooming.

Beginning with an overview of Florida's historical background, the author proceeds to take the reader on a "drive along Florida's" highways, pinpointing areas of interest enroute. Realistic, colorful drawings bring life and meaning to the text. A simple index on page 32 makes it possible for young readers to use this work as they begin learning reference skills.

350   Bake, William A.   *The Blue Ridge.*   Viking, 1977.   (J, S)
        112p.

Continuity—one's roots, so to speak—and a feeling for what one can do with the world: these are the offerings of the Blue Ridge Mountains.

From the crest of Brasstown Bald in north Georgia to the northernmost West Virginia ridge above the Potomac, the author follows the Blue Ridge mountain chain through the Great Smokies and the Appalachians. Artistic, color photographs bring the wide vistas and natural wonders of the region to the reader, while historical backgrounds and ecological truths are vividly presented in the very readable text. An informative chapter is devoted to the techniques and equipment needed in photographing nature of this magnitude. A list of references provides additional sources of information and addresses for parks, wilderness areas, and recreational activities are also given.

351   Bealer, Alex W.   *Only the Names Remain: The*   (J, S)
Cherokees and the Trail of Tears.   Illus. by William
Sauts Bock.   Little, 1972.   84p.

> In each Cherokee village there was also a peace chief, and this was
> always a woman.

This book recounts the history of the Cherokees, their first meet-
ings with white settlers and how they learned to work with them. It
includes the development of the Cherokee alphabet by Sequoyah and
the betrayal of the Cherokees by Andrew Jackson.

352   Bell, Thelma Harrington, and Bell, Corydon.   *States*   (I, J, S)
of the Nation: North Carolina.   Coward McCann,
1970.   128p.

> At a cabin fireplace a Cherokee squaw cooks ancestral foods such as
> fragrant bean bread, dried pumpkin, and yellow jacket soup.

The informational material included in this comprehensive overview of the Tarheel State is presented in such a readable fashion and
illustrated so entertainingly with current photographs that it should be
of interest to readers of all ages. The authors have introduced people
and places from the Outer Banks, across the industrial Piedmont, to
the vacation areas of the Great Smoky Mountains; incorporating fascinating reminders of the early pioneers, pirates, and mountaineers with
today's story of universities, industries, and agriculture. A ready-refer-
ence section is included as well as a comprehensive index and several
maps.

353   Bleeker, Sonia.   *The Cherokee: Indians of the*   (I)
Mountains.   Illus. by Althea Karr.   Morrow, 1952.
159p.

> If only these letters could be made to fit the Cherokee language . . .
> then his people could talk on paper too.

The Cherokees lived in the mountains of southeastern America
and their life-style, customs, and beliefs developed before the coming
of the white man. Included are Sequoya's development of a written
language, the uniting of the Cherokee nation, the enforced march into
exile, and mention of present-day life. The book is well illustrated, including maps of the territory, and it is indexed.

354   Bleeker, Sonia.   *The Seminoles.*   Illus. by Althea   (I, J)
Karr.   Morrow, 1954.

> No one spoke, since the Indians have no word in their language for
> good-by.

In graphic, story form the author describes the movement of a village of Creek Indians forced to move to Florida in the early 1800s. On this beginning, she builds the history of the Seminoles (people who go to another country), ending with a description of the three Florida Seminole reservations as they were operated in the 1950s. Excellent black-and-white sketches picture many of the less familiar scenes described in the text. A comprehensive index is included.

355   Bolton, Clyde.   *The Basketball Tide: A Story of*   (J, S)
      Alabama Basketball.   Illus.   Strode, 1977.   242p.

> Covering Alabama basketball is fun and work . . . the story that follows is not a "history" in the musty sense of the word.

This is a story, not so much of the statistics of the Crimson Tide basketball records as of the people involved in the program. Much of this recounting is told by the players and coaches themselves. An appendix gives detailed statistics. The photographs, mostly action shots, add a special dimension to the work.

356   Bolton, Clyde.   *Bolton's Best: Stories of Auto Racing.*   (J, S)
      Illus.   Strode, 1975.   144p.

> My most enjoyable, most fulfilling professional moments have been spent in the press boxes of race tracks. . . .

This collection of stories of the great racing men emphasizes the human interest aspects of their lives. There is a visit with a figure-eight driver who raced trains to the crossing for fun, and a driver whose side line is flipping cars for Hollywood racing movies.

357   Bolton, Clyde.   *War Eagle: A Story of Auburn Football.*   (J, S)
      Illus.   Strode, 1973.   320p.

> Our team went out to the grounds on a street car.

The beginning of Auburn football is given as the game against Georgia in Atlanta in 1892—a very different scene from today's super productions. The colorful story of Auburn's football history includes a foreign bowl game played in Havana, Cuba, as well as chapters devoted to interviews with outstanding players and famous coaches. Many historic photographs and innumerable statistics about the Auburn Tigers are included.

358   Boylston, Elise Reid.   *Atlanta—Its Lore, Legends*   (J, S)
      and Laughter.   Foote and Davies, 1968.   238p.
      (Dist. by Atlanta, Ga. Humane Society)

> Marthasville was then just a wide place in the road where the Indian trails met.

Marthasville later became the city of Atlanta. This book is a very readable history of the city. It recreates the colorful characters and happenings of Atlanta's past and gives an idea of its struggles and its triumphs. Of particular interest to the non-Atlantian are the chapters on Stone Mountain, Andrew's Raid, the Cyclorama, and Coca-Cola.

359   Burgess, Robert F.   *They Found Treasure.*   Dodd,   (S)
           1977.   187p.

> Their cone-shaped sand hole in the ocean bottom suddenly seemed to sprout gold coins.

What kind of people are treasure hunters? How do they find and recover treasure, and what do they do with it? In a series of personal interviews, successful modern day treasure hunters describe their work and its results. Emphasis is on the Spanish treasure ships wrecked in the waters around Florida, but some other areas are included as well. Technical, archaeological, and legal aspects of treasure diving are all discussed. Many photographs, maps, and drawings help make this a fascinating and informative book.

360   Burney, Eugenia.   *Colonial North Carolina.*   (I, J)
           Nelson, 1975.   176p.

> North Carolinians had a right to be proud of their statehouse. Tryon's Palace . . . has often been considered one of the most beautiful government houses in America.

This easy-to-read account of colonial North Carolina traces its history from Walter Raleigh's earliest settlement along the Outer Banks in the 1580s to 1789 when North Carolina became the twelfth state of the Union. Well illustrated with photographs, drawings, and maps, the book presents the many aspects of the state's growth and development in vivid episodes. An extensive bibliography; a list of dates, each identified with a brief description of its importance; a list of historical sites, each with a paragraph on its importance; and a comprehensive index make this excellent resource material.

361   Campbell, Elizabeth.   *Jamestown: the Beginning.*   (I)
           Illus. by William Sauts Bock.   Little, 1974.   86p.

> And ours to hold,
> VIRGINIA,
> Earth's only Paradise.

The vivid descriptions of sea travel in the seventeenth century and the splendid land of Virginia create a setting suitable for the great human adventure of settling a new colony. This account of the first year of Jamestown is accurate yet highly readable, and the pen, ink, and wash drawings help bring the text alive. A list of the Jamestown colonists of 1607 is included.

362 Capps, Clifford Sheats, and Burney, Eugenia.   (I, J)
Colonial Georgia. (Colonial Histories)   Nelson,
1972. 176p.

> By the time Christopher Columbus discovered America, Georgia had been populated for ten thousand years. . . .

It is with a description of these earliest inhabitants that *Colonial Georgia* begins. This interesting and formal history ends as Georgia becomes a part of the new United States. The wealth of detail and many photographs and maps will fascinate readers who enjoy exploring the formative years of the state. Helpful appendixes include Bibliography, Important Dates, and Historic Sites as well as a detailed index.

363 Carr, Archie. *The Everglades.* (The American   (J, S)
Wilderness Series)   Time-Life Books, 1973.   184p.

> The staying power of tide-zone mangroves has saved people as well as coastline.

In text that at times reads like poetry, the author covers the entire region of southern Florida known as the Everglades, describing the flora and fauna of each region and giving both historical backgrounds and ecological implications of the area. Should that prove more than the reader wishes to know about the subject, one can turn to the breathtakingly beautiful colorplates gathered from several of the foremost photographic artists of the country and thus gain a visual image of the area. Included in "An Audubon Sampler" are full-page reproductions of nine of the artists' most famous paintings of birds native to the Everglades. A bibliography and comprehensive index add to the reference value of the work.

364 Cate, Herma; Ussery, Clyde; and Armstrong, Randy.   (J, S)
The Southern Appalachian Heritage.   Holston, 1974.   op
94p.

> Young Mandy could hardly close her eyes for thinking of the long day's adventure ahead.

Eye-catching, full-color photographs enrich the poetic-prose statements which recount the trek of the first white settlers to their homes in the Southern Appalachian Mountains. Life-styles, education, religion, music, crafts, and folktales are all treated briefly but succinctly. The final section records various ways in which descendants of those early settlers are now preserving their heritage for future generations. Included are such topics as the apple wagons of Cades Cove, Decoration Day activities, childrens' chores, porch swings, corn patches, recipes of long ago, and a description of the final yearly harvest on a typical mountain farm.

365 Cate, Margaret Davis. *Our Todays and Yesterdays.* (J, S)
A Story of Brunswick and the Coastal Islands. Rev. op
ed. Grover Bros., 1930. 302p. (Reprint ed.,
Reprint Co., 1972)

> The scene just beyond the house . . . was beautiful; the moonlight slept on the broad river . . . and on the masses of foliage of the giant southern oaks. . . .

This history of the coastal region of Georgia covers the period from colonial beginnings to 1930. It contains stories, reminiscences, and documents, making it a very readable text with abundant biographical materials. Maps, a good index, and photographs add to its usefulness.

366 Caulfield, Patricia. *Everglades.* Sierra Club, (S)
1970. 143p.

> The mangrove begins where the sawgrass and cypress heads stop.

This elegant, oversize volume may prove too expensive for the average young person's library. However, the artistic full-color photographs, the selections from the writings of Peter Matthiessen which accompany them, the essay on the historical background and ecosystem of the Everglades by John G. Mitchell, and the thought provoking introduction by Paul Brooks make this book well worth its price. A two-page full-color map provides an added resource for study of the area.

367 Conger, Ledie William. *Sketching and Etching* (J, S)
Georgia. Text by Ruth Dunlop Conger. Conger
Print. Co., 1971. unp.

> The front garden retaining the original hour glass pattern. . . .

The above quotation illustrates the appeal of Mrs. Conger's descriptions of the fifty lovely etchings and drawings contained in this volume. The facts used in describing the homes and other points of interest are told, as the artist sketched, to the writer of the text by occupants or other authorities. Some of the homes and buildings are open daily to the public and visitors are welcome. All can be admired through this lovely tribute to the Congers' adopted home state of Georgia.

368   Curto, Josephine. *Biography of an Alligator.* Illus.   (P, I)
      by Bill Elliott.   Putnam, 1976.   64p.

>   Night settled over the Everglades. The baby alligator listened to the booming "jug-o-rum" of a frog. . . .

He had begun the day as an egg in the nest, had hatched, entered the water, and learned to catch his food. In the days and years which follow, he survives the many dangers of the wild and comes to maturity. A simple text and realistic black-and-white drawings portray the ecology of the Everglades as they present the life story of an alligator. A brief epilogue describes the history of the alligator as an endangered species.

369   Dabney, Virginius. *Virginia, the New Dominion:*   (S)
      a History from 1607 to the Present.   Doubleday, 1971.
      629p.   (Paperback ed., Doubleday, 1971)

>   I have sought in the present work to bring together . . . the Virginia story.

Tracing Virginia's history from the first settlement at Jamestown through the leadership provided to the Revolution, the tragedy of the Civil War and the developments of the twentieth century, this represents the best single-volume history of Virginia available. Emphasis is placed on the contributions of blacks, Germans, and other groups. Virginia's twentieth-century leaders are well represented. A bibliography and index are included.

370   Davis, Burke. *Appomattox: Closing Struggle of the*   (I, J)
      Civil War.   Ed. by Walter Lord.   (A Breakthrough
      Book)   Harper, 1963.   167p.

>   On a hot Palm Sunday afternoon . . . the bloodiest war in American history came to an end.

This detailed account covers the events leading to and including Lee's surrender to Grant at Appomattox. Correspondence between the two generals and terms of surrender are included. This work may well be compared to MacKinlay Kantor's *Lee and Grant at Appomattox.* A biliography and excellent period photographs are included.

371   Dean, Blanche E.   *Ferns of Alabama and Fern*   (J, S)
      Allies.   Illus.   American Southern, 1964.   232p.

>   The flora of Alabama is unsurpassed by any of the surrounding states with the possible exception of North Carolina.

This book gives the places where the different kinds of ferns may be found in Alabama. It includes a description and a clear drawing of each type of fern. There is a good bibliography and index.

372   Debo, Angie.   *The Rise and Fall of the Choctaw*   (S)
      Republic.   Univ. of Oklahoma Pr., 1972.   314p.

>   In 1826, United States commissioners held a council with the Choc-
>   taws at Florence, Alabama. . . .

The history of the Choctaw Indians, a proud and gifted tribe
among the five civilized tribes of Indians, is closely interwoven with
the larger fabric of American history. Included are events in the life
of the tribe, their customs, schools, churches, and economic institutions.

373   Dodd, Donald B.   *Historical Atlas of Alabama.*   (I, J, S)
      Cartography by Borden Dent.   Univ. of Alabama Pr.,
      1974.   173p.

>   Alabama is a Choctaw word meaning "thicket clearers or vegetable
>   gatherers."

The narrative introductions to each chapter summarize the year
and synthesize the basic patterns of the maps. The focal points in time
that are treated are 1860, 1900, 1930, and 1970. However, some other
years are included to show the effects of war, depression, or other significant factors.

374   Douglas, Marjory Stoneman.   *The Everglades: River*   (S)
      of Grass.   Illus. by Robert Fink.   Hurricane House,
      1947.   406p.

>   . . . they have always been, one of the unique regions of the earth,
>   remote, never wholly known.

Other volumes treat the natural and human history of southern
Florida in a more scholarly or scientific manner than this book, but
none surpasses its literary quality or depth of appreciation for the subject. Published just as the Everglades National Park was coming into
existence, the assessment of ecological needs is outdated only in detail.
The basic problems and their causes remain as described. Essential
reading for any serious student seeking an introduction to the nature
and needs of the region.

375   Douglas, Marjory Stoneman.   *Florida: the Long*   (S)
      Frontier.   (Regions of America Series)   Harper,
      1967.   307p.

>   A Spaniard screamed as a fire-hardened reed arrow penetrated his
>   chain armor. . . .

Thus the Florida Indians attacked the men of Ponce de Leon,
driving them away and ending the first European attempt to settle
Florida in 1521. Much of Florida was to remain a frontier until well

into the twentieth century. Mrs. Douglas traces Florida history from its geological formation to the 1960s. This is one of the most thorough of the nonscholarly histories of the state, enjoyable both for its style and its attention to less well-known developments, such as Florida's involvement in the Civil War. An extensive bibliography is given.

376   Evans, Lawton B.   *A History of Georgia for Use in*   (J, S)
          Schools.   Rev. ed.   American Bk., 1908.   357p.   op
          (Reprint ed., Reprint Co., 1972)

> Quick as thought the dauntless woman sprang to the guns, jerked one up, cocked it, and with an oath. . . .

This quotation illustrates the very good short summaries of the important periods in Georgia history included in this work. The treatment is chronological: early explorers, Georgia under trustees, Georgia under royal governors, as an independent state, in the Federal Union, in the Confederacy, Reconstruction times, and re-entry into the Union. It includes questions and topics for discussion at the end of each chapter. Good illustrations including maps and portraits as well as a detailed index are included.

377   Fager, Charles E.   *Selma, 1965*.   Illus.   Scribner,   (S)
          1974.   241p.

> As the early months of 1965 unfolded, the dialectic of old and new in white Selma was to become more complex—almost beyond recognition.

In 1965 Selma, Alabama, is the site chosen for a massive voter rights demonstration by local blacks and northern whites. This book reconstructs the struggle and the eventual march to Montgomery to confront Governor George Wallace with a demand for enfranchisement. Dominating the picture are Martin Luther King and President Lyndon Johnson.

378   Fancher, Betsy.   *Savannah: a Renaissance of the Heart*.   (S)
          Doubleday, 1976.   157p.

> Among scions of the aristocracy, almost anything could provoke a duel. . . .

Savannah is a charming city with beautiful squares, splendid mansions, fine restaurants and taverns. The author provides not only a history of this lovely city but a guide, illustrated with photographs, to the present-day scenes as well.

379   Fishwick, Marshall W.   *Jamestown: First English*   (I, J, S)
          Colony.   (American Heritage Junior Library)   op
          American Heritage, 1965.   151p.

Boldness was one weapon that won Virginia for the English.

How the brave, bold English colonists led by Captain John Smith secured a foothold in America is the subject of this well illustrated account. Plans for colonization, actual settlement of the Roanoke and Jamestown colonies, the discovery of tobacco, relations with the Indians and the leaders who held the colony together are all covered. A variety of illustrations add interest to this well known story.

380 Fleming, Thomas J. *The Battle of Yorktown.*   (I, J)
     (American Heritage Junior Library)   American
     Heritage, 1968.   153p.

I propose a cessation of hostilities . . . to settle terms for the surrender of the posts at York and Gloucester.

Cornwallis was trapped. Prodded by the French, Washington abandoned New York, marched south to Virginia, and attacked Cornwallis at Yorktown. Unable to break the siege; the troops decimated by illness, casualties, and desertion; the British surrendered October 17, 1781. Army life and personalities on both sides are well documented in illustrations as is the French naval victory over the British in Chesapeake Bay. A bibliography and index are included.

381 *Florida, A Picture Tour.*   Introduction by Richard   (J, S)
     Powell.   Scribner, n.d.   160p.

When something stood in the way of progress, like too much water, one removed it.

Powell's perceptive and entertaining historical essay sets the stage for an outstanding collection of over 150 photographs, including many magnificent color plates. This pictorial trip covers more than 800 miles from Pensacola to Dry Tortugas. Along the way one sees great cities and small villages, monuments and industries, wilderness and tourist meccas, farmland and beaches, wildlife and technology, the old and the new, the famous and the obscure. The great variety of the state becomes apparent in this comprehensive look at Florida and its heritage.

382 Foshee, John H.   *Alabama Canoe Rides and Float*   (J)
     Trips.   Illus.   Strode, 1976.   263p.

This book is written from a canoeist's viewpoint but it's not just for canoe or kayak or foldboat. . . .

A detailed guide to the Cahaba and twenty-five other creeks and rivers of Alabama, the book also contains locations of put-ins, take-outs, and other general information about numerous streams in the state.

383 Garrett, Milchell B. *Horse and Buggy Days on*   (J, S)
  Hatchet Creek. Univ. of Alabama Pr., 1964. 233p.   op

> As I sat musing on a broken sill of the old mill dam—the idea of writing a book someday . . . began to take shape in my mind.

This story takes place in the 1880s and early 1890s. Times are hard but the farmers eat well, enjoy revivals, log-rollings, weddings, foot-washings, swimming in the millpond, and trips to town. This is a delightful book about a little-known way of life in long-ago America.

384 Goerch, Carl. *Ocracoke.* Illus. by "Primrose."   (I, J)
  Blair, 1956. 223p.

> It just naturally feels good to walk through the sand, barefooted.

A "folksy" picture of experiences and scenes which the author encountered while visiting the island during the 1950s is supplemented by attractive line drawings which add to the realistic tone of the work. Simple discussions are given on such subjects as fishing, recreational opportunities, interesting personalities, and weather.

385 Hall-Quest, Olga W. *Jamestown Adventure.* Illus.   (I, J)
  by James MacDonald. Dutton, 1950. 185p.   op

> Inspired by new courage and new resolutions and a deep faith, the Jamestown adventure carried on.

The first twelve years of the Jamestown colony are tragic years. The tiny settlement maintained only a shaky hold in its poorly selected location. Death was always present in one form or another. Disease, starvation, and Indians threatened to destroy the colony. Captain John Smith's efforts to communicate and trade with the Indians and his explorations of the area are described. The story, based on original documents, is authentic and its events are vividly detailed.

386 Hamilton, Virginia Van de Veer. *Alabama: A*   (J, S)
  Bicentennial History. Illus. (The States and the
  Nation Series) Norton, 1977. 189p.

> The editor of this series requested a somewhat different kind of history. . . .

Following the direction of the editors, the author creates a different history of Alabama than that usually found in textbooks or chronological accounts of long-ago events. This history reflects upon the mind, spirit, and outlook of Alabamians through the years. An interesting approach which makes for fascinating reading.

387 Hannum, Alberta Pierson. *Look Back with Love.*   (J, S)
  Vanguard, 1969. 205p.

This is a personal remembrance of a time that was, and perhaps will never be again.

Interspersed with artistic black-and-white photographs, these essays are bits and pieces of the author's recollections of the time she spent in the Blue Ridge Mountains, teaching at Crossnore (N.C.) School. Chapter headings, taken exactly from old Uncle Jake's diary, may prove difficult for some readers since spelling and punctuation follow his own ideas, but they add much to the flavor and vigor of the work.

388 Harris, Joel Chandler. *Stories of Georgia.* Rev. ed. (J, S)
American Bk., 1896. 315p. (Reprint eds., Reprint Co. op
1972; Cherokee Pubs., 1971)

The old South made new by events; the old South with new channels . . . the old South with new possibilities of greatness.

These twenty-seven Georgia history stories and anecdotes by the author of the famous Uncle Remus stories, were originally intended for use in the schools and were arranged in one volume so as to form a series of connecting links in the rise and progress of Georgia. The book contains such chapters as Liberty Boys, Yazoo Fraud, Cotton Gin, Creeks and the Creek War, Two Famous Indian Chiefs, Slavery and Secession, Great Locomotive Chase, and many others. It also has a new introduction by the leading Harris scholar—Thomas H. English of Emory University, Atlanta, Georgia.

389 Harwell, Richard. *Margaret Mitchell's "Gone with* (S)
the Wind" Letters: 1936–1949. Macmillan, 1976.
441p.

My world was going to explode some day, and God help me if I didn't have some weapon to meet the new world.

Thus wrote Margaret Mitchell in one of the ten thousand letters contained in this book. Between sudden fame and untimely death she sometimes considered writing a second novel—about the loss of her privacy when her first one became a best seller. Had she written such an autobiographical novel, Miss Mitchell might have had difficulty producing a more effective depiction of that period of her life and work than is contained in this collection of her letters.

390 Hemphill, Paul. *The Good Old Boys.* Anchor, (S)
1975. 280p.

Growing up is, of course, in line with the prevailing notion, a terrifying experience.

A collection of newspaper and magazine stories written about the South during the 1960s and early 1970s, filled with humor and local color, bring to life an era in the South that is fading.

391   Imhof, Thomas A. *Alabama Birds.* 2nd ed. Illus.   (S)
      Univ. of Alabama Pr., 1976.   445p.

   One of the best ways to see birds is to attract them to the home.

In a comprehensive guide to bird study, Alabama birds are grouped and classified according to the scientific categories of order, suborder, family, subfamily, and genus. Also included is a glossary, topography patterns of bird migration, and other aids in locating species. The colored illustrations assist in more accurate identification of birds. Types of bird feeders are also described.

392   Jahoda, Gloria. *The Other Florida.* Scribner, 1967.   (S)
      336p. (Paperback ed., Scribner Florida Classics   op
      Library, 1978)

   North Florida, like the south in general . . . turned its attention to becoming a working part of America.

Traveling "west-to-east-to-south," the author explores north Florida from Pensacola to Saint Augustine to Cedar Key—interviewing local characters, enjoying the local color of "off-tourist" areas, reveling in the beauties of nature, and delving into the historical backgrounds of both places and industries. The reader is given a realistic picture of the locale as well as a "good feeling" about its inhabitants and their problems. The vivid journalistic style makes for easy reading and the many photographs add to the readers' involvement in the material.

393   Jahoda, Gloria. *River of the Golden Ibis.* Illus. by   (S)
      Ben F. Stahl, Jr.   Holt, 1973.   408p.

   For at least ten thousand years men have lived on the Hillsborough
   River and Tampa Bay.

Savages, conquistadores, missionaries, pirates, settlers, soldiers, immigrants, capitalists, retirees: all made their mark on the region now publicized as Florida's suncoast. Here is their story, from the Paleo-Indians and Hernando DeSoto to Henry Plant and Doc Webb. Human history is interwoven with natural history, as climate, topography, and natural resources have attracted these people, and as they have in turn made their mark on the land, the water, and the air. Novelistic style makes for enjoyable as well as informative reading. There is an extensive bibliography.

394   Jones, Kenneth M.   *War With the Seminoles, 1835–*   (J, S)
      1842. Watts, 1975. 86p.

The Indians soon discovered the deception, and raids and massacres
again became prevalent.

Based on the author's research on the Seminole wars while working for a master's degree at Stetson University in Deland, Florida, this
definitive account of the wars, their causes, and conclusions is an important resource for the serious student of Florida history. The text
is well illustrated with authentic photographs from such sources as
the American Museum of Natural History and the Library of Congress.
Also included are several full-page reproductions of portraits of
Seminole leaders painted by the famous artist, George Catlin. A selected bibliograph and a five-page index add to the book's usefulness
as a reference tool.

395   Kantor, MacKinlay.   *Lee and Grant at Appomattox.*   (I, J)
      Illus. by Donal McKay. (Landmark Books) Random,
      1950. 175p.

This was Friday, the seventh of April, 1865. It wouldn't be long now.

The beginning of the end of Civil War was at hand. General
Grant and General Lee were only a few miles apart and only a few
days apart was the surrender and signing of the truce at Appomattox
that ended the war. This is a detailed portrait of those last days, showing Lee and Grant and the two opposing armies and events that closed
the war. This account covers the same material as Burke Davis' book
Appamattox: Closing Struggle of the Civil War.

396   Kollock, John.   *These Gentle Hills.*   Copple House   (J, S)
      Books, 1976. 112p.

You must approach them slowly, sit awhile with them and learn their
ways.

Thus the color and soft-spoken charm of the Blue Ridge Mountains of Georgia are captured by the artist-author. Here the special
magic of the seasons is interwoven with history and nostalgia. The
drawings and paintings capture many scenes which have passed away,
as well as existing and familiar landmarks.

397   Lane, Mills.   *Savannah Revisited: a Pictorial History.*   (J, S)
      Beehive Pr., 1973. 160p.

Today visitors can still revisit the city's past by walking through the
oasis squares of the first settlement. . . .

The reader can do almost the same in this handsome volume

which records vividly in words and pictures the transformation of a poor and unhappy eighteenth-century military outpost into a rich and prosperous nineteenth-century world port. For a halcyon 100 years Savannah was a cotton capital, a place to be traded with and reckoned with. This book is a rare documentary record, with more than 150 illustrations of old city views, maps, and architectural photographs. It also presents a good view and understanding of the present-day restored Savannah.

398 Langford, George. *The Crimson Tide, Alabama* (J, S)
Football. Illus. Regnery, 1974. 218p.

Success is not a definition, it is a constant, continuous journey.

The University of Alabama's success on the gridiron is recounted in a very readable way with many anecdotes and illustrations. A complete record of the coaches, captains, and scores of the games played since 1892 is included.

399 Laumer, Frank. *Massacre!* Univ. of Florida Pr., (S)
1968. 188p.

. . . agony-twisted fingers clutching at the sand and blood flowing like tears from a hundred wounds.

On December 28, 1835, the troopers of the command of Major Francis Dade died in a massacre which began the long and bitter Second Seminole War in Florida. This painstakingly researched account of the battle and the events leading up to and following it reads like a novel. The suspenseful march of the doomed column, the noise and horror of the conflict, the heroic desperation of the trapped soldiers, and the dispassionate efficiency of the victors bring history to life as a real and human story.

400 Lawson, Marie. *Pocahontas and Captain John Smith:* (I)
The Story of the Virginia Colony. Illus. by William op
Sharp. Random, 1950. 185p.

How stubborn these white men were!

The first permanent English settlement in the New World began as a dream of Sir Walter Raleigh. Beginning with that dream, this history includes the attempted settlement on Roanoke Island, the hardships of the Jamestown colonists, the colonists' relationships with the Indians, and the first Virginia wedding. This interesting and easy-to-read story ends with the outcome of Bacon's Rebellion and the building of Williamsburg in 1698.

401   Levenson, Dorothy.   *The First Book of the Civil War.*   (P)
Illus.   Watts, 1968.   74p.

> Now there were two Presidents: one in Washington and one in Montgomery.

This very simple book of the Civil War, beginning with the inauguration of Abraham Lincoln and going through the surrender at Appomattox, has many uses for students. It will introduce younger students to this historical period, or serve as resource material for the older student with reading problems. Original Civil War drawings and photographs add to its appeal.

402   Lineback, Neal G.   *Atlas of Alabama.*   Univ. of   (J, S)
Alabama Pr., 1973.   138p.

> We hope this book will help its readers to recognize the state's potential and to obtain a more realistic image of Alabama.

A description of the physical, cultural, and economic characteristics of Alabama utilizing maps, graphs as well as interesting text makes this an appealing atlas. It is useful as a reference tool and as a means of better understanding the relationship between man and the land. Charles T. Traylor serves as cartographic director for the work.

403   Lockerman, Doris, and LaHatta, Patricia.   *Discover*   (J, S)
Atlanta.   Simon and Schuster, 1969.   252p.

> Clearly, this city was a late bloomer, but it was born running.

The authors explain the essence and spirit of Atlanta and at the same time provide an extensive guide to the city. The most important parts of the book are the chapters History of Atlanta and The Whole State. However, the excellent writing and interesting facts make exciting reading for the native, the visitor, or anyone wishing to know more about this fascinating city. It is well illustrated with photographs and maps.

404   Lovell, Caroline Couper.   *Golden Isles of Georgia.*   (S)
Little, 1932.   300p.   (Reprint ed., Cherokee Pr., 1970)   op

> The island was . . . beautifully wooded . . . Its forests of oak and pine were interspersed with open savannas. . . .

Although this was written about one of the golden isles of Georgia, it could be a description of any of them. Add to these woodlands and savannas the ocean and its beaches, the marshes and evidences of past history, and find the past and current appeal of these lovely isles. The book is devoted primarily to the early history of the area and its importance in the history of Georgia and the South.

405   Lyon, Ernest.   *My Florida.*   Illus. by James   (J, S)
          Hutchinson.   Barnes, 1969.   226p.   op

   I saw a picture of home the other day that I will never forget.

   Home for journalist Lyon is the area around Stuart, Florida. These sketches from his column in Stuart's semi-weekly newspaper celebrate the Florida he has known and loved for over half a century. It is not the Florida of tourists, super highways, and condominiums, but the Florida of birds and animals, the wilderness, and the pioneer settlers. The book presents a charming, somehow hopeful, picture of a natural paradise and a simple way of life which are being unalterably changed by progress and development.

406   McMillan, Malcolm C.   *Yesterday's Birmingham.*   (J, S)
          Illus. (Seemann's Historic Cities Series #18)
          Seeman, 1976.   208p.

   The history of the New South city of Birmingham and its metropolitan area from its birth, in 1871, to the middle 50's. . . .

   The development of the coal and iron industry in Birmingham is the main theme of this work. Along with the industrial growth of the city is included the development of the social and political life of Birmingham. This book about Alabama's largest city will be of interest not only to Jefferson County residents but also to students throughout the state.

407   Martin, Clarence.   *Roswell, Historic Homes and*   (J, S)
          Landmarks: a Collection of Drawings by Ernest E.
          DeVane.   Roswell Historical Society, 1967.   unp.

   Major Bullock did not live to see the marriage of his daughter Mittie to Theodore Roosevelt. . . .

   The volume depicts fourteen scenes in Roswell, Georgia, an old historic town just outside of Atlanta. The drawings are lovely and the text adequately describes the beauty and historic significance of the home or outdoor location.

408   Mikell, Isaac Jenkins.   *Rumbling of the Chariot*   (S)
          Wheels.   State Printing Co., 1923.   273p.   op

   "A little more speed, Andrew, more speed!" my father would call out.

   The author reminisces about plantation life during his boyhood on Edisto Island and the Low Country of South Carolina. Also included are incidents that occurred when Sherman marched through the state during the Civil War. Many places of interest in the state are briefly described in this book.

409   Morris, Allen,' ed.   *The Florida Handbook, 1979–1980.*   (J, S)
17th ed.   Peninsular Pub. Co., 1979.   660p.

Many of Florida's modern highways have as their origin ancient Indian trails.

Up-to-date information on Florida's government, natural resources, and famous personalities is included in this latest edition of the *Florida Handbook*. Published biannually, it has, through the years, become an important reference tool for anyone interested in Florida affairs. Brief, well-written historical background essays are given for subjects which lend themselves to this approach. Photographs, maps, and numerical tables add to the interest of the material. A copy of the 1968 revision of the Florida State Constitution is included, as well as a comprehensive index to the entire volume.

410   Newman, Zipp.   *The Impact of Southern Football.*   (S)
M.B. Publishing, 1969.   297p.

You're dealing with an authority and a historian, and maybe most of all, a fan. . . .

The colorful story of Alabama and southern football, the players who went on to national fame and glory, unfold before the eyes of the reader in this exciting account, written from the viewpoint of a sports writer.

411   Parks, Pat.   *The Railroad That Died at Sea.*   Stephen   (J, S)
Greene Pr., 1968.   44p.

Key West Extension, a single-track Florida shortline . . . , met death by hurricane on September 2, 1935.

That part of the Florida East Coast Railway popularly known as the Overseas Railroad took twelve years to build and was considered one of the engineering marvels of the world. Henry Flagler's most ambitious undertaking, it operated for only twenty-three years; but it opened the wilderness of the Florida Keys to development, and its roadbed and bridges form the basis for today's Overseas Highway. This is its story, readable, well researched, and generously illustrated with photographs; a unique chapter in the annals of American railroading.

412   Perkerson, Medora Field.   *White Columns in Georgia.*   (S)
Rinehart, 1952.   367p.

Old houses never quite give up the people who have lived within their walls.

The history and legends of Georgia antebellum mansions are

described so interestingly that this book is almost a leisurely visit through the state. The author has an eye for the homes' present beauty and an ear for the legends that through the years have clustered around them. Her choice of houses is varied, and the story of Georgia's white columns matches the social history of the state itself. The book is beautifully illustrated with photographs and has a good index.

413 Powell, William S. *North Carolina.* Watts, 1966.   (I, J)
92p.

The people of North Carolina were once as varied in their origins, language and interests as is the geography of the state.

Designed to give the intermediate student a brief overview of North Carolina, this work presents brief chapters on the physical characteristics, history, people, economics, educational opportunities, and tourist attractions of the Tarheel state. Recent black-and-white photographs add interest to the text. An excellent index increases the usefulness of the material.

414 Powell, William S. *North Carolina: A Bicentennial*   (S)
History. Photographs by Bruce Roberts. (The States
and the Nation Series) Norton, 1977. 221p.

By 1860 most North Carolinians realized that trouble was brewing and that there was little they could do to avoid it.

In this work Powell presents a scholarly account of the historical background of North Carolina from the early 1700s to the present time. Written in his usual readable style, the material is well documented with many footnotes. A comprehensive index makes this a most useful reference tool, and the "Suggestions for Further Reading" is a helpful guide for the more serious student. Sensitive black-and-white photographs present a visual essay on North Carolina as it is today.

415 Ramsey, Robert W. *Carolina Cradle: Settlement of*   (S)
the Northwestern Carolina Frontier, 1747–1762.
Univ. of North Carolina Pr., 1964. 251p.

Two of the early landowners in the Fourth Creek settlement lived elsewhere in North Carolina.

This definitive study of Rowan County, an area of the North Carolina frontier lying between the Yadkin and Catawba rivers, attempts to trace the ways in which this part of the southern Piedmont was populated. To do this, the author studied the various records left by the early settlers in order to identify them, their reasons for emigrating to this area, and the ways in which they organized the frontier community. The work is well documented and indexed. Numerous maps add to the value of the information given. This work is a valuable reference tool as well as a fine historical study.

416 *Rivers of Alabama.* Illus. by Jack B. Hood. Strode, (J, S)
1968. 211p.

> Nine well-known writers and water enthusiasts combine their efforts to present a systematic coverage of a waterway system such as Alabama's . . . .

Each of the major rivers of Alabama is described by a different writer. These are the waterways which have historical significance as well as economic value to the state. Lesser river systems are covered as they relate to these nine major ones. A map and a good index leads the user to significant facts about the rivers and the areas through which they flow.

417 Roberts, Nancy. *The Goodliest Land: North Carolina.* (I, J, S)
Photographs by Bruce Roberts. Doubleday, 1973.
175p.

> No one ever dashed into an old-fashioned general store to make a purchase.

Eye-catching black-and-white photographs coupled with equally descriptive word-pictures are used in this portrayal of the Tarheel state. The authors travel from the stormy shores of Cape Hatteras to the western ridge of the Great Smokies relating historical events, providing glimpses of famous personalities, and picturing the life-styles of another era in an effort to capture the true spirit of this area. The final chapter, "Can We Keep the Goodliest Land?" is a plea for ecological reform and preservation of the natural resources of this beautiful region.

418 Romine, Dannye. *Mecklenburg: A Bicentennial Story.* (J, S)
Independence Square Associates, 1975. 84p. op

> Mecklenburgers, along with the other colonists, chafed under the yoke of British rule.

Using a series of anecdotes, gleaned from extensive research, the author brings to life many important people, places, and events that helped shape the first two hundred years of history of Charlotte and Mecklenburg County, North Carolina (1753–1974). The reproductions of original intaglios, done by the well-known printmaker, Donald R. Sexauer, introduce each segment of the historical journey and add depth and flavor to the text. An extensive bibliography as well as a list of original source material is included.

419   Rouse, Parke, Jr.   *Virginia, a Pictorial History.*   (J, S)
Scribner, 1975.   358p.

> Earth's only Paradise.

Parke Rouse, Jr., a native Virginian, pictures the state from the settlement at Jamestown to the 1970s. The pictures, with a commentary for each, give an accurate and concise story of Virginia's history. This work portrays the Virginians' love of the land, their participation in the wars, and their many contributions to the country.

420   Scruggs, Carroll Procter.   *Georgia from Plum Orchard*   (I, J, S)
to Plum Nelly.   Bay Tree Grove Pubs., 1971.   63p.

> Huge dunes guard the wind-gnarled live oaks which shelter the playground of white-tailed deer.

Thus the author describes Cumberland Island—the location of Plum Orchard, one of the Carnegie family homes unfortunately destroyed by fire and now owned by the National Parks Foundation. The volume, designed as a pictorial sampler, describes places, scenes, and homes from the islands of southeast Georgia to Plum Nelly in the mountains of northwest Georgia. Beautifully illustrated with color photographs, the book is, in the words of the author, "for the youngsters, who have time to dream, and for the oldsters, who have time to travel."

421   Sheppard, Muriel Earley.   *Cabins in the Laurel.*   (S)
Photographs by Barry Wooten.   Univ. of North
Carolina Pr., 1965.   313p.

> They've gone by themselves now, and the worst we got to put up with is being lonesome.

In the foreword the reader learns that "as the wife of a mining engineer stationed widely in Appalachia" in the twenties and thirties, the author became engrossed in the historical backgrounds, cultural patterns, and folkways of her mountain neighbors. Using the oral history approach she collected material for this work—interviewing old settlers, some of whom remembered Civil War days. In this way she "tapped memories which went back into uninvaded mountain country, recreating play parties and quilting bees, and not omitting the gusto which for some found outlet in the whiskey jug and for others in the revival meeting." The Toe River Valley of North Carolina is the area from which the material was gathered. The episodes are recounted sometimes in pictorial prose and sometimes in the ballad form so often used by the hill folk. The coverage is wide including early railroading, exploration, and early settlements on now familiar mountain sites, mining both for gems and gold, and a wealth of local folklore and customs. Excellent photographs add much to the well-written text.

422   Sibley, Celestine. *Place Called Sweet Apple.* Illus.   (S)
by Ray Cruz. Doubleday, 1967. 240p.

> Sun struck the white oak boards of the roof just to bring out the
> weathered silver in them.

Sweet Apple is a restored log cabin which serves as the author's
home. It is located in rural north Georgia within easy driving distance
of Atlanta. The book describes Mrs. Sibley's experiences and her impressions of the area. Of particular delight is her account of the seasons as they unfold. It contains many recipes of the area and is well
indexed.

423   Smith, Robert Sellers. *Alabama Law for the Layman.*   (J, S)
Illus. Strode, 1975. 304p.

> It is hoped the information in this book will help you to understand
> the nature of Alabama law. . . .

The first four chapters deal with Alabama civil laws, the next
two with criminal law, and the remainder tell of the court system in
Alabama. Written in simple language for students and lay readers,
this book includes a good glossary and index.

424   Smith, Scottie Fitzgerald. *An Alabama Journal,*   (J, S)
1977. Strode, 1976. 112p.

> This journal is the result of my earnest effort to get to know this
> [Alabama] fabulous land of my forebears.

This attractive combination of history, recipes, and photographs
of the unique places in Alabama traces tradition and customs from the
very old to the modern life-style. Billy Noble was picture editor for
this well executed work.

425   Stabler, Kenneth Michael, with LaMarre, Tom. *Ken*   (J, S)
Stabler's Winning Offensive Football. Regnery, 1976.
180p.

> I wouldn't trade my football days for anything in the world.

This fairly technical book on football is interspersed with personal anecdotes from Ken Stabler's football days with the Foley,
Alabama, *Lions* to the University of Alabama *Crimson Tide* and later
with the *Raiders.* An introduction by Paul ("Bear") Bryant adds to
the authenticity of the material covered.

426   Stevenson, Janet. *The Montgomery Bus Boycott,*   (J, S)
*December, 1955: American Blacks Demand an End to
Segregation.* Illus. Watts, 1971. 63p.

I had no intention of doing any such thing when I got on the bus.

This account tells the story of the boycott strictly from the point of view of the black man. Pictures throughout the book bear cutlines that, if read, can give a younger or poorer reader a feeling of having read the book. Helpful features include a paragraph synopsis of the work and a listing of the principals involved in the story. An index makes the book useful as a reference tool.

427 Stick, David. *The Outer Banks of North Carolina,* (J, S)
1584–1958. Univ. of North Carolina Pr., 1958.
352p.

One of the most common misconceptions about the Outer Banks is the belief that commercial fishing has been the primary occupation and source of income in the area since the days of earliest settlement.

The Outer Banks is not only a distinct section of North Carolina geographically, but its people have an independent way of life and culture. The author recounts the history of this fascinating region from its discovery by the explorers to the present resort developers. "Bankers," whalers, pirates, tourists, aviators, and fishermen all had a vital role in the development of the region. The last chapter, "The Banks Today," includes a short description of each of the Banks communities and other points of interest. References and sources are appended.

428 Stockton, Frank R. *Buccaneers and Pirates of Our* (I, J, S)
Coasts. Macmillan, 1956. 325p.

The buccaneers of America differed in many ways from those pirates . . . of the old world. . . .

This highly readable account of the famous and infamous sea-robbers who plundered North American coasts from the sixteenth to the nineteenth centuries includes Jean Lafitte, Henry Morgan, Blackbeard, and Captain Kidd, plus several less well known pirates. Considerable material is drawn from the writings of John Esquemeling, himself a pirate-turned-author. Since this is a long-time favorite work, several different editions of it may be found.

429 Tunis, Edwin. *Shaw's Fortune: the Picture Story of a* (P, I)
Colonial Plantation. Crowell, 1976. 63p.

This book is about the way people lived then around the Chesapeake Bay.

Shaw's Fortune is described as it developed from a log cabin in 1630 to a large and almost self-sufficient plantation in 1752. Everyday life and work including crafts, tobacco farming, and education are re-created through the text and the detailed drawings of Edwin Tunis. This record of 150 years of plantation living, although for younger children, is useful for older students and adults because of the well-researched and accurate illustrations.

430   Turner, Sue.   *Bouquets, Brambles and Buena Vista, or*   (J, S)
       "Down Home."   Strode, 1976.   128p.

> The Alabama Historical Commission in 1976 presented *Down Home* its award of merit. . . .

This collection of the weekly columns written for the *Monroe Journal*, Monroeville, Alabama, about the author's hometown of Buena Vista is filled with humor, human interest, and nostalgia. The accounts could have taken place in any rural area of Alabama.

431   Van Noppen, Ina W., and Van Noppen, John J.   (S)
       Western North Carolina Since the Civil War.
       Appalachian Consortium Pr., 1973.   437p.

> Western North Carolina was never a land apart from the rest of the state, even in the earliest days, in spite of the mountain barrier.

The northwestern region of North Carolina has undergone changes in the last hundred years which have had wide-ranging effects on the life-styles of its people. The Van Noppens have combined traditional resources, personal interviews, and local research in this comprehensive work which covers the economic, political, and social development of the area following the Civil War. Also included is a section on the folklore and customs of the mountain people. The text is informative and readable. The index is very useful in locating specific information. Footnotes originally included by the authors have been deleted to make the work more readable, but their sources, including the names or persons interviewed, are appended.

432   Walker, Alyce Billings, ed.   *Alabama, A Guide to the*   (J, S)
       Deep South.   Rev. ed.   (American Guide Series)
       Hastings House, 1975.   411p.

> Since publication of the original *Guide* Alabama has passed through a period of vast social change.

This valuable reference book contains the history of the state and a description of the major cities of the state. It includes sixteen tours of the state, giving a detailed description of each trip. The appendix includes a chronology, bibliography, index to map sections, maps, and an index.

433   Walker, Anne Kendrick.   *Tuskegee and the Black Belt.*   (J, S)
Illus.   Diety Pr., 1944.   unp.

> The Tuskegee Choir . . . made its debut at the opening of Radio City. . . .

Subtitled "A Portrait of a Race," this work traces the development of Tuskegee Institute. Located in the heart of Alabama's Black Belt, it has from the very beginning stressed education, agricultural improvement, health, and justice. The story of Booker T. Washington, founder, is woven into the story. The introduction by the Hon. Chauncey Sparks, then Governor of Alabama, and the many paintings and photographs included add much to the worth of the work.

434   Walser, Richard, and Street, Julia Montgomery.   (I, J)
North Carolina Parade.   Illus. by Dixie Burrus
Browning.   Univ. of North Carolina Pr., 1966.   209p.

> Not all of the people of North Carolina were eager for independence from Great Britain.

The more than thirty sketches in this volume take the reader through North Carolina history from the story of Virginia Dare of the "Lost Colony" to the establishment of the Research Triangle Park in 1959. This "parade" of history was especially designed and recorded in short, readable episodes to interest teenagers just beginning their study of their North Carolina heritage. Attractive black-and-white line drawings illustrate these interesting "stories of history and people."

435   Walton, George.   *Fearless and Free: The Seminole*   (S)
Indian War 1835–1842.   Bobbs-Merrill, 1977.   274p.

> They saw the major slump in his saddle and slowly, almost gracefully, fall to the ground.

The massacre of Major Dade and his command in December, 1835, began what is now known as the Second Seminole War. This scholarly and well-written history of the conflict presents it as basically a defense of slavery, and reveals that it was as controversial at the time as the Vietnam War was in its day. The political maneuverings at home proved as crucial as the maneuverings of the battlefields, and few of the commanders involved kept their reputation intact in this "dirty little war of aggression."

436   Wetmore, Ruth Y.   *First on the Land: The North*   (J, S)
Carolina Indians.   Blair, 1975.   196p.

> In some areas conch shells may have been attached to stick handles and used as hoes.

The author, curator of the Indian Museum of the Carolinas at Laurinburg, has gathered information about the Indian tribes of North Carolina from many sources and has presented it in an interesting, readable style that should interest students and help them better understand and appreciate their Indian neighbors. The book is illustrated with attractive photographs, loaned by various historical collections across the state. A list of references, by chapter, is included as well as a detailed index.

437   Williams, George Walton.   *The Best Friend.*   Illus.   (P, I)
by John Kolluck.   Berg, 1969.   unp.

It was the first locomotive built in America for service on a railroad.

Called the "Best Friend," the little locomotive was to provide the answer to the economic crisis which Charleston was experiencing due to a lack of transportation for cotton. A track was laid from Charleston to Hamburg, across the river from Augusta, Georgia. The fireman's carelessness brought about the early demise of the first engine, but it was replaced by the "Phoenix," which continued to bring prosperity to the Charleston merchants and ushered in the Railroad Age in America. Humorous line drawings add to the effectiveness of this book for younger readers.

438   Williford, William Bailey.   *Peachtree Street, Atlanta.*   (S)
Univ. of Georgia Pr., 1962.   176p.

. . . reminder of the gentle beauty of the past and of the magnificent promise of the future. . . .

Both of these are ever present along world famous Peachtree Street, Atlanta. In telling the story of the street, naturally the history of the city is related. Anyone interested in Georgia or Atlanta will enjoy this informational book. There are numerous photographs of houses, buildings, and outstanding people. In addition, a bibliography and index are included.

439   Wimberly, Christine Adcock.   *Poisonous Snakes of*   (I, J, S)
Alabama.   Illus. by Tom De Jarrette.   Explorer
Books, n.d.   46p.

In Alabama, deaths from poisonous snake bites are four to five times the national average. . . .

A thorough treatment of the four poisonous snakes of Alabama, this work is a *must* for Alabama youngsters. Rhymes are given to help identify the coral which is the only poisonous snake which is not a pit viper. Shapes, with color patterns, are given as ways of recognizing these poisonous species. First-aid techniques as well as ways of avoiding snakes are discussed. The drawings are humorous and instructive. Dr. William J. Pitts's photographs are excellent.

440 Windham, Kathryn Tucker. *Alabama: One Big Front*   (J, S)
Porch. Illus. by H. Roland Russell. Strode, 1975.
157p.

> Alabama, they say, is like one big front porch where folks gather on summer nights to tell tales and talk family.

A collection of tales of politics and of war, of families and of old friendships, includes also some superstitions and some typically Southern recipes. A few Alabama heroes make their appearance as well as some scoundrels and reprobates.

441 Windham, Kathryn Tucker. *Exploring Alabama.*   (J, S)
Strode, 1970. 252p.

> The most amazing things happen in Alabama.

Readers interested in learning more about the early history of Alabama will enjoy this book which tells of those people who first lived in the area, focussing on both explorers and pioneers. It also traces the political structure, giving an account of the formation of state government through the Reconstruction period.

442 Windham, Kathryn Tucker. *Treasured Alabama*   (J, S)
Recipes. Illus. by Diane Hamilton Sampson. Strode,
1967. 115p.

> Wherever you are, take two (biscuits, that is) and butter them while they're hot . . . you'll be eating Alabama style.

The recipes of this cookbook are divided into six regional areas, with traditions and descriptions typical of each area included. Seafood is the specialty on the coast, while in the piney woods fish and game along with vegetables are special. In the wire-grass country, peanuts and other high calorie dishes are important parts of the diet. The Black Belt is the home of folks who treasure their heritage of gracious living and the Tennessee Valley area brings together a blend of the new and the old. Up in the Appalachian range the farmers grow the state's finest produce, which has been used to advantage for the table. A comprehensive index is divided into types of recipes.

443 Wright, Louis B. *Barefoot in Arcadia: Memories of a*   (S)
More Innocent Era. Univ. of South Carolina Pr.,
1974. 175p.

As for horses, give me a mule or a jackass any day.

With freshness and charm, Louis Wright cleverly avoids cliches in this exaltation of small-town life in South Carolina in the first part of this century. The author uses anecdote, description, and good-natured philosophizing to portray a wise and literate people, whose ecological concerns grew out of intimate contact with the land and who conducted their business, social, and legal affairs with the common sense which abides only in a true respect for human nature. The author maintains that we have lost the capacity to adequately deal with life's joy and tragedy because we have removed ourselves from firsthand experiences and primary human relationships—from which we receive our truest education.

444 Young, Joanne. *Spirit Up the People: North Carolina* (S)
—The First Two Hundred Years. Photographs by
Taylor Lewis, Jr. Oxmoor House, 1975. 152p.

The object of this detachment is to . . . spirit up the people.

Lavishly illustrated with color photographs which show the unforgettable beauty of North Carolina from the Outer Banks on the eastern Atlantic coast to the majestic Blue Ridge Mountains on the west, this fast-moving account of the early history of the state brings life and vigor to the early settlements as well as to revolutionary and colonial activities. The author enlivens historical facts with interesting, but accurate, anecdotes about such colorful figures as Blackbeard and his pirates; the patriot ladies of Edenton, who staged their own "tea party," and General Daniel Morgan, who outsmarted the British leader, Tarleton. Photographs of homes, plantations, and villages give a taste of the architecture of the times and of the work done by the talented craftsmen of the period. The work is well indexed and lists historical sources used.

STATE LISTS

The State Lists provide for each state in the region an author-title key, arranged by category, to the books listed, indicating by number their location in the Annotated Bibliography. If a book pertains to more than one state, it appears in the listing for each. Reading level is indicated in parentheses following each title.

ALABAMA

FICTION

6   Baughman, Dorothy. *Piney's Summer.* (P, I)
23   Brown, Joe David. *Paper Moon.* (J, S)
24   Brown, Marion Marsh. *The Silent Storm.* (I, J)
26   Brown, Virginia Pounds. *The Gold Disc of Coosa.* (I)
36   Burton, Herbert. *Adventures of Dixie North.* (I)
37   Butterworth, W. E. *Dateline—Talladega.* (I, J)
45   Coleman, Lonnie. *Orphan Jim.* (J, S)
52   Davis, Harwell Goodwin. *The Legend of Landsee.* (J)
78   Hamilton, Betsy. *Southern Character Sketches.* (J, S)
116   Lee, Harper. *To Kill a Mockingbird.* (J, S)
118   Lee, Mildred. *The Rock and the Willow.* (I, J)
119   Lee, S. C. *Little League Leader.* (I, J)
128   Maddox, Hugh. *Billy Boll Weevil.* (P)
129   Mason, David P. *Five Dollars a Scalp: The Last Mighty War Whoop of the Creek Indians.* (J)
133   Milton, Hilary. *November's Wheel.* (I, J)
137   Olsen, Theodore. *There Was a Season.* (S)
152   Pyrnelle, Louise-Clarke. *Diddie, Dumps and Tot: or Plantation Child-Life.* (I, J)
163   Scholefield, Edmund O. *Yankee Boy.* (J)

164 Searcy, Margaret Zehmer. *Ikwa of the Temple Mounts.* (J)
177 Snow, Dorothea J. *The Secret of the Stone Frog.* (I)
178 Sorensen, Virginia. *Curious Missie.* (I)
182 Stewart, John Craig. *Muscogee Twilight.* (J, S)
187 Tate, Allen. *Jefferson Davis, His Rise and Fall: A Biographical Narrative.* (J, S)
190 Thompson, Wesley S. *So Turns the Tide.* (S)
197 Wellman, Manly Wade. *Young Squire Morgan.* (I)

FOLKTALES

230 Scott, Flo Hampton. *Ghosts with Southern Accents and Evidence of Extrasensory Perception.* (J, S)
233 Windham, Kathryn Tucker and Figh, Margaret Gillis. *13 Alabama Ghosts and Jeffrey.* (I, J, S)

POETRY, DRAMA, MUSIC

234 Glass, Paul, and Singer, Louis C. *Songs of Hill and Mountain Folk: Ballads, Historical Songs.* (J, S)
236 Harwell, Richard B. *Confederate Music.* (J, S)
237 Henderson, Rosamon. *The Epic: The Battle of Horseshoe Bend.* (J, S)

BIOGRAPHY AND PERSONAL ACCOUNTS

244 Aaron, Henry. *Aaron.* (J, S)
250 Avant, D. A. *Like a Straight Pine Tree: Stories of Reconstruction Days in Alabama and Florida 1885–1971.* (J, S)
252 Bigland, Eileen. *Helen Keller.* (I, J)
264 Daly, Robert Walter. *Raphael Semmes: Confederate Admiral.* (J, S)
269 Davidson, Margaret. *Helen Keller.* (P)
275 Einstein, Charles. *Willie Mays: Coast to Coast Giant.* (I, J)
278 Foster, John. *Southern Frontiersman: The Story of General Sam Dale.* (I)
279 Frady, Marshall. *Wallace.* (J, S)
282 Goodrum, John C. *Wernher von Braun: Space Pioneer.* (J, S)
283 Graff, Steward, and Graff, Polly Anne. *Helen Keller: Toward the Light.* (P, I)
284 Graham, Shirley. *Booker T. Washington: Educator of Hand, Head and Heart.* (I, J)
285 Graham, Shirley, and Lipscomb, George D. *Dr. George Washington Carver, Scientist.* (I, J)

287 Green, Margaret. *President of the Confederacy: Jefferson Davis.* (J, S)

294 House, Jack. *Lady of Courage: The Story of Lurleen Burns Wallace.* (S)

295 Huie, William Bradford. *He Slew the Dreamer. . . .* (J, S)

296 Jackson, Robert E. *Joe Namath, Superstar.* (I, J)

298 Judson, Clara Ingram. *Soldier Doctor: The Story of William Gorgas.* (P, I)

300 Krementz, Jill. *Sweet Pea: A Black-girl Growing Up in the Rural South.* (P, I)

302 Libby, Bill. *Ken Stabler, Southpaw Passer.* (J, S)

305 Marks, Henry S. *Who Was Who in Alabama.* (J, S)

308 Meriwether, Louise. *Don't Ride the Bus on Monday: The Rosa Parks Story.* (I)

310 Milverstedt, F. M. *The Quiet Legend: Henry Aaron.* (I, J)

315 Radford, Ruby L. *Sequoya.* (P)

316 Randall, Ruth Painter. *I Varina: . . . .* (J, S)

318 Sayers, John W. *Who's Who in Alabama.* (J, S)

319 Sloan, Steve. *Calling Life's Signals: The Steve Sloan Story.* (J, S)

322 Smith, Ken. *The Willie Mays Story.* (J, S)

323 Snow, Dorothea J. *Raphael Semmes: Tidewater Boy.* (P, I)

326 Starr, Bart, with Cox, Max. *Bart Starr Quarterbacking.* (J, S)

329 Stevenson, Augusta. *Booker T. Washington: Ambitious Boy.* (P, I)

333 Underwood, John. *Bear, The Hard Life and Good Times of Alabama's Coach Bryant.* (J, S)

335 Wallace, Cornelia. *C'Nelia.* (S)

336 Wallace, George. *Stand Up for America.* (J, S)

337 Wallace, George, Jr. *The Wallaces of Alabama: My Family.* (J, S)

340 Walters, Helen B. *Wernher von Braun: Rocket Engineer.* (J, S)

344 Williams, Beryl, and Epstein, Samuel. *William Crawford Gorgas: Tropical Fever Fighter.* (I, J)

OTHER INFORMATIONAL BOOKS

346 Akens, Helen Morgan, and Brown, Virginia Pounds. *Alabama Mounds To Missiles.* (I, J)

351 Bealer, Alex W. *Only the Names Remain: The Cherokees and the Trail of Tears.* (J, S)

355 Bolton, Clyde. *The Basketball Tide: A Story of Alabama Basketball.* (J, S)

356   ————. *Boltons Best: Stories of Auto Racing.* (J, S)

357   ————. *War Eagle: A Story of Auburn Football.* (J, S)

371   Dean, Blanche E. *Ferns of Alabama and Fern Allies.* (J, S)

372   Debo, Angie. *The Rise and Fall of the Choctaw Republic.* (S)

373   Dodd, Donald B. *Historical Atlas of Alabama.* (I, J, S)

377   Fager, Charles E. *Selma, 1965.* (S)

382   Foshee, John H. *Alabama Canoe Rides and Float Trips.* (J, S)

383   Garrett, Milchell B. *Horse and Buggy Days on Hatchet Creek.* (J, S)

386   Hamilton, Virginia Van de Veer. *Alabama: A Bicentennial History.* (J, S)

390   Hemphill, Paul. *The Good Old Boys.* (S)

391   Imhof, Thomas A. *Alabama Birds.* (S)

398   Langford, George. *The Crimson Tide, Alabama Football.* (J, S)

401   Levenson, Dorothy. *The First Book of the Civil War.* (P)

402   Lineback, Neal G. *Atlas of Alabama.* (J, S)

406   McMillan, Malcolm C. *Yesterday's Birmingham.* (J, S)

410   Newman, Zipp. *The Impact of Southern Football.* (S)

416   *Rivers of Alabama.* (J, S)

423   Smith, Robert Sellers. *Alabama Law for the Layman.* (J, S)

424   Smith, Scottie Fitzgerald. *An Alabama Journal, 1977.* (J, S)

425   Stabler, Kenneth Michael, with LaMarre, Tom. *Ken Stabler's Winning Offensive Football.* (J, S)

426   Stevenson, Janet. *The Montgomery Bus Boycott, December, 1955: American Blacks Demand an End to Segregation.* (J, S)

430   Turner, Sue. *Bouquets, Brambles and Buena Vista, or "Down Home."* (J, S)

432   Walker, Alyce Billings, ed. *Alabama, A Guide to the Deep South.* (J, S)

433   Walker, Anne Kendrick. *Tuskegee and the Black Belt.* (J, S)

439   Wimberly, Christine Adcock. *Poisonous Snakes of Alabama.* (I, J, S)

440   Windham, Kathryn Tucker. *Alabama: One Big Front Porch.* (J, S)

441   ————. *Exploring Alabama.* (J, S)

442   ————. *Treasured Alabama Recipes.* (J, S)

FLORIDA

FICTION

3   Ball, Zachary. *Salvage Diver.* (I, J, S)

5 Bannon, Laura. *When the Moon is New: a Seminole Indian Story.* (P, I)
14 Blassingame, Wyatt. *The Golden Geyser.* (S)
22 Brothers, Betty. *Triggerfish: Tales of the Florida Keys.* (J, S)
38 Butterworth, W. E. *The Roper Brothers and Their Magnificent Steam Automobile.* (J, S)
39 Caras, Roger. *Panther!* (J, S)
46 Corcoran, Barbara. *A Dance to Still Music.* (J, S)
48 Cotten, Nell. *Piney Woods.* (I, J)
50 Cummings, Betty Sue. *Let a River Be.* (J, S)
58 Farley, Walter. *The Black Stallion's Ghost.* (I, J, S)
68 Francis, Dorothy B. *Nurse of the Keys.* (I, J)
69 _____. *Run of the Sea Witch.* (I, J)
76 Hall, Rubylea. *Davey.* (I, J)
77 _____. *The Great Tide.* (S)
82 Haskins, Ida. *Adventures on the Airboat Trail.* (I, J)
85 Hays, Wilma Pitchford. *Siege! The Story of St. Augustine in 1702.* (I, J)
87 Heatter, Basil. *"Wreck Ashore!"* (J, S)
92 Hoff, Syd. *Irving and Me.* (I, J)
93 Holding, James. *The Mystery of Dolphin Inlet.* (J, S)
94 Holland, Marion. *No Children, No Pets.* (I)
95 Hooker, Ruth, and Smith, Carole. *The Pelican Mystery.* (P, I)
96 Hunt, Irene. *The Lottery Rose.* (J, S)
97 Hurston, Zora Neale. *Jonah's Gourd Vine.* (S)
98 Ironmonger, Ira. *Alligator Smiling in the Sawgrass.* (P, I)
104 Knudson, R. R. *You Are the Rain.* (J, S)
106 Konigsburg, E. L. *(George).* (I, J)
113 Lawrence, Mildred. *One Hundred White Horses.* (I, J)
114 _____. *Sand in Her Shoes.* (P, I)
117 Lee, Mildred. *Honor Sands.* (J, S)
122 Lenski, Lois. *Strawberry Girl.* (I, J)
123 Lippincott, Joseph W. *The Phantom Deer.* (I, J)
124 _____. *The Wahoo Bobcat.* (I, J)
125 Ludman, Barbara. *The Strays.* (J, S)
126 McNeer, May. *Bloomsday for Maggie.* (J, S)
143 Powell, Richard. *I Take This Land.* (S)
144 Prather, Ray. *Anthony and Sabrina.* (P)
145 Pratt, Theodore. *The Barefoot Mailman.* (S)
146 _____. *The Big Bubble.* (S)
148 Price, Eugenia. *Don Juan McQueen.* (J, S)
150 _____. *Maria.* (S)

153 Rawlings, Marjorie Kinnan. *The Secret River.* (P, I, J, S)
154 _____. *The Yearling.* (I, J, S)
168 Shelton, William R. *Stowaway to the Moon: the Camelot Odyssey.* (S)
171 Slaughter, Frank G. *Apalachee Gold.* (J, S)
183 Stolz, Mary. *Lands End.* (I, J)
192 Vinson, Kathryn. *Run With the Ring.* (S)
193 Waldron, Ann. *The Luckie Star.* (I, J)
201 Wier, Ester. *The Winners.* (I, J, S)

FOLKTALES

227 Newell, David M. *If Nothin' Don't Happen.* (S)

BIOGRAPHY AND PERSONAL ACCOUNTS

245 Alderman, Clifford L. *Osceola and the Seminole Wars.* (J, S)
274 Egypt, Ophelia Settle. *James Weldon Johnson.* (P, I)
276 Felton, Harold W. *James Weldon Johnson.* (I, J)
290 Harner, Charles E. *Florida's Promoters: The Men Who Made It Big.* (J, S)
291 Hartley, William, and Hartley, Ellen. *Osceola, the Unconquered Indian.* (S)
320 Smiley, Nixon. *Crowley Tales.* (J, S)
332 Syme, Ronald. *Osceola: Seminole Leader.* (I, J)

OTHER INFORMATIONAL BOOKS

349 Bailey, Bernadine. *Picture Book of Florida.* (P, I)
354 Bleeker, Sonia. *The Seminoles.* (I, J)
359 Burgess, Robert. *They Found Treasure.* (S)
363 Carr, Archie. *The Everglades.* (J, S)
366 Caulfield, Patricia. *Everglades.* (S)
368 Curto, Josephine. *Biography of an Alligator.* (P, I)
374 Douglas, Marjory Stoneman. *The Everglades: River of Grass.* (S)
375 _____. *Florida: the Long Frontier.* (S)
381 *Florida, A Picture Tour.* (J, S)
392 Jahoda, Gloria. *The Other Florida.* (S)
393 _____. *River of the Golden Ibis.* (S)
394 Jones, Kenneth M. *War With the Seminoles, 1835–1842.* (J, S)
399 Laumer, Frank. *Massacre!* (S)
405 Lyon, Ernest. *My Florida.* (J, S)
409 Morris, Allen, ed. *The Florida Handbook, 1979–1980.* (J, S)

411 Parks, Pat. *The Railroad That Died at Sea.* (J, S)
435 Walton, George. *Fearless and Free: The Seminole Indian War 1835–1842.* (S)

GEORGIA

FICTION

2 Armstrong, William H. *Sounder.* (I, J)
10 Beim, Lorraine. *Triumph Clear.* (I, J)
13 Blackburn, Joyce. *Suki and the Magic Sand Dollar.* (P, I)
27 Burch, Robert. *D. J.'s Worst Enemy.* (I)
28 ———. *Hut School and the Wartime Home-front.* (I)
29 ———. *Queenie Peavy.* (I, J)
30 ———. *Renfroe's Christmas.* (I)
31 ———. *Simon and the Game of Chance.* (I)
32 ———. *Skinny.* (I)
33 ———. *Tyler, Wilkin, and Skee.* (I)
34 Burchard, Peter. *Bimby.* (I)
47 Cormack, Maribelle. *Swamp Boy.* (I, J)
109 Latham, Jean Lee. *The Story of Eli Whitney.* (I)
134 Mitchell, Margaret. *Gone With the Wind.* (J, S)
136 Oertel, Theodore E. *Jack Sutherland: a Tale of Bloody Marsh.* (J, S)
147 Price, Eugenia. *Beloved Invader.* (S)
148 ———. *Don Juan McQueen.* (S)
149 ———. *Lighthouse.* (S)
151 ———. *New Moon Rising.* (S)
156 Rockwood, Joyce. *Long Man's Song.* (I, J)
158 St. John, Wylly Folk. *The Christmas Tree Mystery.* (I)
159 ———. *The Ghost Next Door.* (I)
160 ———. *The Secret of the Seven Crows.* (I)
161 ———. *The Secrets of the Pirate Inn.* (I)
162 ———. *Uncle Robert's Secret.* (I)
169 Sibley, Celestine. *Christmas in Georgia.* (I, J, S)
172 Smith, Doris Buchanan. *Kelly's Creek.* (I)
173 ———. *Kick a Stone Home.* (I, J)
174 ———. *A Taste of Blackberries.* (I)
175 ———. *Tough Chauncey.* (I, J)
199 Whitney, Phyllis A. *Lost Island.* (J, S)
202 Wilkinson, Brenda. *Ludell.* (I, J)

FOLKTALES

212   Brookes, Stella Brewer. *Joel Chandler Harris: Folklorist.* (S)
220   *Foxfire 2.* (J, S)
224   Killion, Ronald G., and Walker, Charles T. *A Treasury of Georgia Folklore.* (J, S)
232   Windham, Kathryn Tucker. *Thirteen Georgia Ghosts and Jeffrey.* (I, J)

POETRY, DRAMA, MUSIC

240   Lanier, Sidney. *Poems of Sidney Lanier.* (J, S)

BIOGRAPHY AND PERSONAL ACCOUNTS

247   Anderson, William. *Wild Man from Sugar Creek.* (S)
254   Blackburn, Joyce. *James Edward Oglethorpe.* (I, J)
255   _____. *Martha Berry.* (I, J)
258   Byers, Tracy. *Martha Berry, the Sunday Lady of Possum Trot.* (S)
314   Radford, Ruby L. *Juliette Low: Girl Scout Founder.* (I)

OTHER INFORMATIONAL BOOKS

348   Atlanta Journal-Constitution. *Georgia Rivers.* (J, S)
353   Bleeker, Sonia. *The Cherokee: Indians of the Mountains.* (I)
354   _____. *The Seminoles.* (I, J)
358   Boylston, Elise Reid. *Atlanta—Its Lore, Legends and Laughter.* (J, S)
362   Capps, Clifford Sheats, and Burney, Eugenia. *Colonial Georgia.* (I, J)
365   Cate, Margaret Davis. *Our Todays and Yesterdays.* (J, S)
367   Conger, Ledie William. *Sketching and Etching Georgia.* (J, S)
376   Evans, Lawton B. *A History of Georgia for Use in Schools.* (J, S)
378   Fancher, Betsy. *Savannah: a Renaissance of the Heart.* (S)
388   Harris, Joel Chandler. *Stories of Georgia.* (J, S)
389   Harwell, Richard. *Margaret Mitchell's "Gone with the Wind" Letters.* (S)
396   Kollock, John. *These Gentle Hills.* (J, S)
397   Lane, Mills. *Savannah Revisited: a Pictorial History.* (J, S)
403   Lockerman, Doris, and LaHatta, Patricia. *Discover Atlanta.* (J, S)
404   Lovell, Caroline Couper. *Golden Isles of Georgia.* (S)

407 Martin, Clarence. *Roswell, Historic Homes and Landmarks.* (J, S)
412 Perkerson, Medora Field. *White Columns in Georgia.* (S)
420 Scruggs, Carroll Procter. *Georgia from Plum Orchard to Plum Nelly.* (I, J, S)
422 Sibley, Celestine. *Place Called Sweet Apple.* (S)
438 Williford, William Bailey. *Peachtree Street, Atlanta.* (S)

NORTH CAROLINA

FICTION

4 Banning, Margaret Culkin. *I Took My Love to the Country.* (S)
7 Beaman, Joyce Proctor. *All For the Love of Cassie.* (J, S)
8 ————. *Broken Acres.* (J, S)
11 Bell Thelma Harrington. *The Two Worlds of Davy Blount.* (I, J)
12 ————. *Yaller-Eye.* (P, I)
18 Bothwell, Jean. *Lady of Roanoke.* (S)
19 Boyd, James. *Drums.* (S)
20 ————. *Old Pines and Other Stories.* (S)
40 Carroll, Ruth, and Carroll, Latrobe. *Beanie.* (P)
43 Cleaver, Vera, and Cleaver, Bill. *Trial Valley.* (J, S)
49 Credle, Ellis. *Down, Down the Mountain.* (P)
51 Davis, Burke. *The Summer Land.* (S)
55 Dykeman, Wilma. *The Tall Woman.* (S)
57 Ehle, John. *The Land Breakers.* (S)
61 Fletcher, Inglis. *Cormorant's Brood.* (S)
62 ————. *Lusty Wind for Carolina.* (S)
63 ————. *Raleigh's Eden.* (S)
64 ————. *Rogue's Harbor.* (S)
65 Forbes, Tom H. *Quincey's Harvest.* (J, S)
71 Gillett, Mary. *Bugles at the Border.* (J, S)
99 Jarrell, Mary. *The Knee-baby.* (P)
105 Koch, Dorothy. *Up the Big Mountain.* (P)
115 Lay, Elery. *Trek to the King's Mountain.* (S)
120 Lenski, Lois. *Blue Ridge Billy.* (I)
127 MacNeill, Ben Dixon. *Sand Roots.* (S)
130 Meader, Stephen W. *Phantom of the Blockade.* (J, S)
138 Owen, Guy. *Journey for Joedel.* (S)
142 Pierce, Ovid Williams. *On a Lonesome Porch.* (S)

155 Roberts, Nancy. *Sense of Discovery: The Mountain.* (P, I)
167 Sharpe, Stella Gentry. *Tobe.* (P, I)
176 Smith, Edith Hutchins. *Drought and other North Carolina Yarns.* (S)
179 Stahl, Ben. *Blackbeard's Ghost.* (I, J)
184 Street, James, and Tracy, Don. *Pride of Possession.* (S)
186 Sutton, Felix. *We Were There at the First Airplane Flight.* (J)
191 Tyler, Anne. *If Morning Ever Comes.* (S)
194 Wellman, Manly Wade. *Battle for King's Mountain.* (S)
195 _____. *Carolina Pirate.* (S)
196 _____. *Settlement on Shocco.* (J, S)
198 West, John Foster. *Appalachian Dawn.* (S)
203 Wilkinson, Sylvia. *Moss on the North Side.* (S)
205 Williams, Maxville Burt. *First for Freedom.* (J, S)
206 Wolfe, Thomas. *Look Homeward, Angel.* (S)

FOLKTALES

208 Arnold, Lattye Eunice. *Aunt Malissa's Memory Jug.* (I, J)
213 Chaney, James A., ed. *Carolina Country Reader.* (S)
214 Chase, Richard, ed. *Grandfather Tales.* (I, J)
215 _____. *Jack and the Three Sillies.* (P)
216 _____. *The Jack Tales.* (I, J)
217 Credle, Ellis. *Big Fraid, Little Fraid.* (P)
218 _____. *Tall Tales from the High Hills.* (J, S)
219 Davis, Burke. *Roberta E. Lee.* (I)
221 Green, Paul. *Home to My Valley.* (I, J, S)
222 Harden, John. *The Devil's Tramping Ground and Other North Carolina Mystery Stories.* (I, J, S)
226 Morgan, Fred T. *Uwharrie Magic.* (J, S)
228 Parris, John. *Mountain Bred.* (J, S)
229 Roberts, Nancy. *Ghosts of the Carolinas.* (J, S)

POETRY, DRAMA, MUSIC

238 Jarrell, Randall. *The Bat-Poet.* (I, J)
241 Pearson, James Larkin. *My Fingers and My Toes.* (I, J, S)

BIOGRAPHY AND PERSONAL ACCOUNTS

261 Clancy, Paul R. *Just a Country Lawyer.* (S)
268 Daugherty, James. *Daniel Boone.* (I, J)
324 Sobol, Donald J. *The Wright Brothers at Kitty Hawk.* (I, J)

330 Stevenson, Augusta. *Virginia Dare: Mystery Girl.* (P, I)
338 Walser, Richard. *The Black Poet.* (S)
339 ———. *Young Readers' Picture Book of Tar Heel Authors.* (J)

OTHER INFORMATIONAL BOOKS

350 Bake, William A. *The Blue Ridge.* (J, S)
352 Bell, Thelma Harrington, and Bell, Corydon. *States of the Nation: North Carolina.* (I, J, S)
360 Burney, Eugenia. *Colonial North Carolina.* (I, J)
364 Cate, Herma, and others. *The Southern Appalachian Heritage.* (J, S)
384 Goerch, Carl. *Ocracoke.* (I, J)
387 Hannum, Alberta Pierson. *Look Back with Love.* (J, S)
413 Powell, William S. *North Carolina.* (I, J)
414 ———. *North Carolina: A Bicentennial History.* (S)
415 Ramsey, Robert W. *Carolina Cradle: Settlement of the North-western Carolina Frontier, 1747–1762.* (S)
417 Roberts, Nancy. *The Goodliest Land: North Carolina.* (I, J, S)
418 Romine, Dannye. *Mecklenburg: A Bicentennial Story.* (J, S)
421 Sheppard, Muriel Earley. *Cabins in the Laurel.* (S)
427 Stick, David. *The Outer Banks of North Carolina, 1584–1958.* (J, S)
431 Van Noppen, Ina W., and Van Noppen, John J. *Western North Carolina Since the Civil War.* (S)
434 Walser, Richard, and Street, Julia Montgomery. *North Carolina Parade.* (I, J)
436 Wetmore, Ruth Y. *First on the Land: The North Carolina Indians.* (J, S)
444 Young, Joanne. *Spirit Up the People: North Carolina—The First Two Hundred Years.* (S)

SOUTH CAROLINA

FICTION

1   Allen, Merritt Parmelee. *Johnny Reb.* (J, S)
9   Beatty, John Louis, and Beatty, Patricia. *Who Comes to King's Mountain?* (J, S)
15 Bodie, Idella. *Ghost in the Capitol.* (I, J)
16 ———. *The Mystery of the Pirate's Treasure.* (I, J)
17 ———. *The Secret of Telfair Inn.* (I, J)

FOLKTALES

POETRY, DRAMA, MUSIC

BIOGRAPHY AND PERSONAL ACCOUNTS

309 Meriwether, Louise. *The Freedom Ship of Robert Smalls.* (P)
317 Robertson, Ben. *Red Hills and Cotton.* (S)
325 Spratt, Barnett. *Miss Betty of Bonnet Rock School, 1864-1865.* (I, J, S)
327 Steele, William O. *Surgeon Trader, Indian Chief, Henry Woodward of Carolina.* (I, J)
328 Sterne, Emma Gelders. *Mary McLeod Bethune.* (J, S)

OTHER INFORMATIONAL BOOKS

408 Mikell, Isaac Jenkins. *Rumbling of the Chariot Wheels.* (S)
428 Stockton, Frank R. *Buccaneers and Pirates of Our Coasts.* (I, J, S)
437 Williams, George Walton. *The Best Friend.* (P, I)
443 Wright, Louis B. *Barefoot in Arcadia.* (S)

VIRGINIA

FICTION

35 Burchard, Peter. *Rat Hell.* (I, J)
41 Cather, Willa. *Sapphira and the Slave Girl.* (S)
42 Choate, Florence, and Curtis, Elizabeth. *The Five Gold Sovereigns.* (J)
44 Coatsworth, Elizabeth. *The Golden Horseshoe.* (I, J)
53 Davis, Paxton. *The Seasons of Heroes.* (S)
54 Dobler, Lavinia. *Glass House at Jamestown.* (I, J)
60 Finney, Gertrude E. *Muskets Along the Chickahominy.* (J, S)
66 Forman, James. *Song of Jubilee.* (J)
67 Fox, John, Jr. *The Trail of the Lonesome Pine.* (S)
70 Gerson, Noel B. *Give Me Liberty.* (S)
72 Glasgow, Ellen. *In This Our Life.* (S)
73 ———. *Vein of Iron.* (S)
75 Haas, Patricia Cecil. *Swampfire.* (I, J)
80 Hamner, Earl, Jr. *The Homecoming.* (J, S)
81 ———. *Spencer's Mountain.* (J, S)
83 Hays, Wilma Pitchford. *Mary's Star.* (I)
84 ———. *The Scarlet Badge.* (I)
88 Henry, Marguerite. *Misty of Chincoteague.* (I)
89 ———. *Sea Star, Orphan of Chincoteague.* (I)
90 ———. *Stormy, Misty's Foal.* (I)
100 Johnston, Mary. *To Have and To Hold.* (J, S)
101 Kane, Harnett T. *The Gallant Mrs. Stonewall.* (S)

FOLKTALES

POETRY, DRAMA, MUSIC

BIOGRAPHY AND PERSONAL ACCOUNTS

262 Commager, Henry Steele, and Ward, Lynd. *America's Robert E. Lee.* (I)

263 Cunliffe, Marcus. *George Washington and the Making of a Nation.* (I, J)

265 Daniels, Jonathan. *Mosby, Gray Ghost of the Confederacy.* (J)

266 ———. *Robert E. Lee.* (I, J)

267 ———. *Stonewall Jackson.* (I, J)

271 Dillard, Annie. *Pilgrim at Tinker Creek.* (S)

272 Eason, Jeanette. *Leader by Destiny.* (J, S)

277 Fleming, Thomas J. *First in Their Hearts.* (I, J)

280 Freeman, Douglas Southall. *Lee of Virginia.* (J, S)

281 Fritz, Jean. *Where was Patrick Henry of the 29th of May?* (P)

284 Graham, Shirley. *Booker T. Washington.* (I, J)

288 Griffin, Judith Berry. *Nat Turner.* (I, J)

289 Haley, Gail E. *Jack Jouett's Ride.* (P)

292 Henri, Florette. *George Mason of Virginia.* (J, S)

297 Judson, Clara Ingram. *George Washington: Leader of the People.* (I)

299 ———. *Thomas Jefferson: Champion of the People.* (I, J)

303 Lisitsky, Gene. *Thomas Jefferson.* (J, S)

306 Martin, Patricia Miles. *Dolley Madison.* (P)

307 ———. *Pocahontas.* (P)

311 Morse, Charles, and Morse, Ann. *Arthur Ashe.* (P, I)

312 Moscow, Henry. *Thomas Jefferson and His World.* (I, J)

313 Nolan, Jeanette Covert. *Yankee Spy, Elizabeth Van Lew.* (I, J)

321 Smith, Bradford. *Captain John Smith.* (J, S)

331 Syme, Ronald. *John Smith of Virginia.* (I, J)

334 Vance, Marguerite. *Martha, Daughter of Virginia.* (I)

341 Washington, Booker T. *Up From Slavery.* (J, S)

342 Wibberley, Leonard. *Man of Liberty.* (J, S)

343 Wilkinson, J. Harvie, III. *Harry Byrd and the Changing Face of Virginia Politics, 1945–1966.* (S)

345 Wilson, Hazel. *The Years Between.* (I, J)

OTHER INFORMATIONAL BOOKS

347 Anderson, Sherwood. *The Buck Fever Papers.* (J, S)

361 Campbell, Elizabeth. *Jamestown: the Beginning.* (I)

369 Dabney, Virginius. *Virginia, the New Dominion.* (S)

370 Davis, Burke. *Appomattox: Closing Struggle of the Civil War.* (I, J)

379 Fishwick, Marshall W. *Jamestown: First English Colony.* (I, J, S)

380 Fleming, Thomas J. *The Battle of Yorktown.* (I, J)
385 Hall-Quest, Olga W. *Jamestown Adventure.* (I, J)
395 Kantor, MacKinley. *Lee and Grant at Appomattox.* (I, J)
400 Lawson, Marie. *Pocahontas and Captain John Smith.* (I)
419 Rouse, Parke, Jr. *Virginia, a Pictorial History.* (J, S)
429 Tunis, Edwin. *Shaw's Fortune.* (P, I)

DIRECTORY OF REGIONAL PUBLISHERS AND LOCAL BOOK SOURCES

The following information is provided to assist the reader in locating publishers not listed in *Books in Print.*

American Southern Publishers
Northport, Alabama 35476

Appalachian Consortium Press
Appalachian State University
Boone, North Carolina 28608

Banner Press
Birmingham, Alabama

Bay Tree Publishers
Valdosta, Georgia 31601

Beehive Press
321 Barnard St.
Savannah, Georgia 31401

John F. Blair, Publisher
1406 Plaza Dr.
Winston Salem, North Carolina 27103

The Book-Keepers Press
2408 Cantebury Rd.
Birmingham, Alabama 35223

Cherokee Publishing Co.
Box 1081
Covington, Georgia 30209

Conger Printing Co.
1619 Chattahoochee Ave., NW
Atlanta, Georgia 30318

Copple House Books
Lakemont, Georgia 30552

The Diety Press, Inc.
Richmond, Virginia

Explorer Books, Inc.
Birmingham, Alabama

Gadsden Publishing Co., Inc.
1180 Noccalula Rd.
Gadsden, Alabama 35976

Gill Printing and Stationery Co.
Mobile, Alabama

Great American Publishing House
Chattanooga, Tennessee 37421

League Press
Montgomery, Alabama

Mickler's Floridiana
Chuluota, Florida 32766
(Specializes in supplying both in- and out-of-print books about Florida)

North Carolina Dept. of Cultural Resources
State Capitol
Raleigh, North Carolina 27611

Oxmoor House—Progressive Farmer
P.O. Box 2463
Birmingham, Alabama 35201

Peninsular Publishing Co.
2503 Jackson Bluff Rd.
Tallahassee, Florida 32304

Reprint Company, Publishers
114-118 Hillcrest Offices
Spartanburg, South Carolina 29301

Roswell Historical Society
Roswell, Georgia 31601

Sayers Enterprises Inc.
2823 Linden Ave.
Birmingham, Alabama 35209

E.A. Seemann Publishing
Box K
Miami, Florida 33156

Selma Printing Inc.
Selma, Alabama 36701

Southern University Press
130 South 19th St.
Birmingham, Alabama 35233

Strode Publishers
7917 Charlotte Dr. S.W.
Huntsville, Alabama 35802

Value Communications, Inc.
11175 Flintkote Ave.
San Diego, California 92121

Wingate Publishers
608 Four Mile Post Rd.
Huntsville, Alabama 35802

AUTHOR-TITLE-SUBJECT INDEX

Authors, titles, and subjects are included in one alphabetical list. Author entries appear in lightface type, subject entries in boldface type, and title entries in italic type. Each entry is followed by at least one boldface number which refers to the entry number assigned to every book listed in the Annotated Bibliography. For a subject entry of a work of fiction, only the entry number of the book is given. For a non-fiction subject entry, the book's entry number is all that is given if the entire book deals with the subject indicated. When only a specific section of the nonfiction book deals with the subject indicated, a colon follows the boldface entry number and the page number or numbers are added in lightface type. When an entry includes more than one reference, a semicolon separates the references.

DATE DUE

Series design by Vladimir Reichl
Composed by FM Typesetting Company in Linotype
Caledonia with Futura Light display faces
Printed on 50# Warren's Olde Style, a pH neutral stock, and
bound by the University of Chicago Printing Department.

88443